Journal of
Early
Childhood and
Infant
Psychology

Volume 4
2008

PACE UNIVERSITY PRESS   NEW YORK

ISSN 1554-6144
ISBN 0-944473-90-3

Address Subscription Inquiries to:

Pace University Press
41 Park Row, Room 1510
New York, NY 10038

www.pace.edu/press
(212) 346-1405

Journal of Early Childhood and Infant Psychology

Editorial Policy: The Journal of Early Childhood and Infant Psychology (JECIP) is a publication of the Association of Early Childhood and Infant Psychologists (AECIP). One aspect of AECIP's mission is to provide a vehicle for networking within early childhood and infant psychology, including fostering research, scholarship, and professional interactions. This journal (JECIP) focuses on publishing original contributions from a broad range of psychological perspectives relevant to infants, young children, parents, and caregivers. Manuscripts incorporating research, theory and applications within clinical, community, development, neurological, and school psychology perspectives are considered. In addition to data-based research, the journal accepts test and book reviews, position statements, literature reviews, program descriptions and evaluations, clinical studies and other professional materials of interest to psychologists working with infants, young children, parents, families, and caregivers.

Format: Manuscripts should be original work not currently submitted for publication to other journals. Authors must follow the guidelines of the Publication Manual of the American Psychological Association (Fifth Edition), and not exceed 30 pages including charts, tables, and references.

Submission: Submit five (5) copies and one (1) floppy disk of the manuscript for editorial review. Avoid including any identifying author information in the text. Selection of manuscripts is based on blind peer review. Include a cover page with the following information: the title of article, author(s) full name(s), title(s), institution of professional affiliations, and mailing and email address of primary author. The cover page will not be sent to reviewers.

Selection Criteria:
• Importance of topic in early childhood and infant psychology
• Accuracy and validity of content
• Contribution to professional practice in early childhood and infant psychology
• Clear and concise writing

Submit manuscripts to the editor at the following address:
Professor Barbara A. Mowder
Editor, JECIP
Psychology Department, Pace University
41 Park Row
New York, New York 10038
Address inquiries to BMowder@pace.edu

Journal of
Early
Childhood and
Infant
Psychology

Volume 4, 2008

**Mini series: Child Care and Relationships: Understanding Relationships
and Relationship Interventions**

*Zeynep Biringen
& Ann Easterbrooks*   1   Child Care and Relationships:
Understanding Relationships and
Relationship Interventions.
An introduction to the Mini-Series

*Carollee Howes &
Sandra Soliday Hong*   4   Early Emotional Availability:
Predictive of Pre-kindergarten
Relationships among Mexican
Heritage Children?

Eva Marie Shivers   27   Using the Emotional Availability
Scales along the Child Care
Continuum

*Zeynep Biringen,
Albertha Moorlag,
Beatrice Meyer, Judi Wood,
Jennifer Aberle,
Shannon Altenhofen, &
Sera Bennett*   39   The Emotional Availability (EA)
Intervention with Child Care
Professionals

Mallary I. Swartz & *M. Ann Easterbrooks*	**53**	Enhancing Parent-Provider Relationships and Communication in Infant and Toddler Classrooms
Ora Aviezer	**75**	Emotional Availability and the Complexity of Child Care: A Commentary

General Articles

Janice H. Kennedy	**83**	Is Maternal Behavior in the Strange Situation Related to Infant Attachment?
Heather Curtiss, *Kathleen Armstrong, & Carol Lilly*	**93**	Positive Behavior Supports and Pediatric Feeding Disorders of Early Childhood: A Case Study
Heather Richard, *Deborah Winders Davis, &* *Barbara M. Burns*	**111**	An Evaluation of the Children's Behavior Questionnaire for Use with Children from Low-Income Families
Erratum	**124**	

Child Care and Relationships:
Understanding Relationships and Relationship Interventions

Guest Editors:
Zeynep Biringen
Colorado State University

Ann Easterbrooks
Tufts University

For millions of children and families, child care is an integral component of their developmental contexts. With large numbers of children experiencing non-maternal child care, issues as well as concerns about children's outcomes are being vigorously discussed in the literature. For example, using the National Institute of Child Health and Human Development (NICHD) data set, Belsky et al. (2007) reported that although parenting was a stronger predictor of children's development than was child care, early child care quantity, quality, and type also were consistent predictors of child outcomes. The papers in this mini-series focus mainly on non-parental child care and the relationships among those involved in child care. Several of the articles use the Emotional Availability (EA) Scales (Biringen, Robinson, & Emde, 1998), as a focal point in their examination of relationships. Additionally, some of the articles highlight interventions aimed at enhancing relationships in child care.

These papers focus on child care and relationships including relationships between parents and their children who are in child care, relationships between children and their child care providers, and relationships between child care providers and parents of children in their care. Where the care takes place (e.g., child care center, family child care home) and the characteristics of the care and care providers may vary. What remains constant is that relationships are a central component of all child care arrangements, whether these relationships are between children and providers, child peers in child care, families and providers, or providers themselves. To paraphrase Winnicott's (1962/1987) statement "there is no such thing as a baby, there is a baby and someone" (p. 88), we might state "there is no such thing as a

All correspondence should be addressed to Zeynep Biringen, Department of Human Development & Family Studies, Colorado State University, Fort Collins, CO 80523. Electronic mail may be sent to biringen@CAHS.Colostate.edu.

child in child care," as children are embedded in a network of relationships among at least three people (i.e., child, provider, family member). This series of papers examines questions about relationships in child care. For example, do relationships between child care providers and very young children predict development at a later date and in another context? Can provider-child relationships be measured using methods developed to assess mother-child relationships? If so, how are home-based assessments applied to child care settings and what are the caveats? Finally, if relationships in child care are integral to children's development, how might they be supported and enhanced?

The first paper, by Howes and Hong examines the relationship between U.S. families of Mexican heritage, child care, and later school adjustment. Using an early version of the EA Scales, 2nd edition, originally developed with dominant culture families, they demonstrate that both the construct of emotional availability, and the EA Scales, appear applicable for this population. The authors highlight the apparent generalizability of several dimensions of mother-child relationships as relevant to non-maternal child care providers. They assert that dimensions of non-maternal care may predict later social competence in children outside of the family setting. Furthermore, they recommend the use of the EA Scales for understanding relationships between child care providers and children.

In the next paper Shivers has done just that, arguing that emotional availability is a core component of relationships between non-parental child care providers and children. Shivers extends the use of the EA Scales by examining the emotional availability of providers in home-based care for infants and young children. In this situation, one provider is caring for multiple children in the home setting. Based on her work, Shivers argues for the importance of using the EA Scales with non-parental caregivers to explore patterns of interactions in the everyday setting of home-based child care. Shivers suggests that the construct of emotional availability assists in understanding the impact of early learning experiences on children's concurrent and future developmental outcomes. Thus, Shivers investigates links between emotional availability and attachment in child care based on the assertion that child care providers can and do serve as important attachment figures for children (Howes, 1999).

The final two contributions explore ways of enhancing relationships in child care. First, Biringen and colleagues investigate the use of the Emotional Availability Intervention for center-based child care providers and the children in their care. The authors describe the intervention and report preliminary findings using the EA Scales and the Attachment Q-Set, suggesting that even though child care providers may be the direct intervention recipients, children may benefit indirectly. Second, Swartz and Easterbrooks focus on provider-parent relationships in center-based child care. Their paper describes the Touchpoints Early Care and Education training, a developmental, relationship-based training to enhance provider-parent relationships and communication (Brazelton & Sparrow, 2006). The authors suggest that such an intervention model may effectively enhance relationships, which are an integral part of young children's social ecological networks. The training appears effective in enhancing parents' perceptions of their relationships with child care providers, especially for parents with less education and lower income. Their findings also suggest that provider continuity may play an important role in child care policies and practices.

Collectively, these papers point to the importance of understanding and building support for relationships (e.g., provider-child, provider-parent) in the context of child care. Taken together, this set of papers offers reflection on the multiple relationships that are important within non-parental child care and offers implications for child care professional development and practice.

References

Belsky, J., Vandell, D. L., Burchinal, M., Clarke-Stewart, K. A., McCartney, K., Owen, M. T., & NICHD Early Child Care Research Network (2007). Are there long-term effects of early child care? *Child Development, 78,* 681-701.

Biringen, Z. (2000). Emotional availability: Conceptualization and research findings. *American Journal of Orthopsychiatry, 70,* 104-114.

Biringen, Z., Robinson, J., & Emde, R. N. (1998). *The Emotional Availability Scales,* 3rd edition, Unpublished manuscript, available from zbiringen@ yahoo.com.

Brazelton, T. B., & Sparrow, J. D. (2006). *Touchpoints.* New York: De Capo Press.

Howes, C. (1999). Attachment relationships in the context of multiple caregivers. In J. Cassidy & P. R. Shaver (Eds.), *Handbook of attachment: Theory, research and clinical applications* (pp. 671-687). New York: Guilford.

Winnicott, D. W. (1962/1987). *The child, the family, and the outside world.* Reading, MA: Addison-Wesley Publishing.

.

Early Emotional Availability: Predictive of Pre-kindergarten Relationships among Mexican-Heritage Children?

Carollee Howes & Sandra Soliday Hong
University of California at Los Angeles

The predictability of scores on the Emotional Availability Scale (EAS) for low-income Mexican-heritage children's relationships with teachers and peers immediately prior to kindergarten entry was examined. Children were observed at home with mothers, in child care at age 3, and in pre-kindergarten at age 4. Complex peer play in pre-kindergarten was associated with age three EAS maternal structuring, but not with EAS maternal sensitivity. Higher EAS involvement scores at age 3 were associated with more pretend play and less exclusion by peers in pre-kindergarten. Children, regardless of child care status, looked similar in mother-child emotional and social relationships at pre-kindergarten. Mothers with lower EAS sensitivity scores who used child care tended to have children with less complex peer play in pre-kindergarten. Children enrolled in child care who had higher maternal EAS structure scores and higher provider scaffolds child play scores tended to have higher pre-kindergarten social competence.

A large body of literature based primarily on dominant culture parents and children in the United States suggests that early mother-child interaction contributes to children's subsequent social competence with teachers and peers (for a review of this literature see Thompson & Raikes, 2003). In general, warmth and sensitivity on the part of the parent and responsive participation on the part of the child during mother-child interactions are associated with children entering formal school ready to form positive relationships with teachers and peers (Biringen, Skillern, Mone, & Pianta, 2005). Biringen and colleagues also found that when mothers engage in a high-level of structuring and sensitivity, children tend to have positive kindergarten social adjustment. Positive mother-child interaction, within the emotional availability schema, has two maternal components: *sensitivity*, the mother's awareness of and responsiveness to the child as well as her ability to express positive affect and

All correspondence should be addressed to Carollee Howes, Department of Education, University of California at Los Angeles, Los Angeles, CA 90095-1521. Electronic mail may be sent to howes@gseis.ucla.edu.

to resolve conflicts; and *structuring*, the mother's ability to structure or scaffold interactions with her child in a sustained manner (Easterbrooks & Biringen, 2000).

The first purpose of the current study was to extend the research on mother and child emotional availability with dominant culture parents and children in the United States to low-income Mexican-heritage parents and children. Mexican-heritage children were defined as children whose mothers or grandmothers were born in Mexico. Although Latino parents are a heterogeneous group, Mexican immigrants are the largest and fastest growing Latino group in the United States. School readiness is important for low-income Mexican-heritage children, in part because of concerns about a mismatch between parental and school expectations of children (Farver, Xu, Eppe, & Lonigan, 2006; Reese, 2002).

Mexican-heritage children, bringing different cultural expectations to schooling than dominant-culture families, may share commonalities with other children whose families are from Mexico and Latin American countries. Latino parents often encourage their children to respect teachers as authority figures and their styles of engagement and interaction around learning may differ from expectations in mainstream kindergarten classrooms (Farver et al., 2006). In general, respectful interactions between Latino adults and children is often described as including more adult direction and control than adult-child interactions in other ethnic groups (Halgunseth, Ispa, & Rudy, 2006).

However, engagement is an important component of school success and includes the ability of the child to use a teacher as a support for learning (La Paro & Pianta, 2000). This type of teacher-child relationship may be particularly important for children at risk for difficult school adjustment, helping to mitigate the downward trajectory associated with poor academic preparation for school (Hamre & Pianta, 2005). Early teacher-child relationships are particularly important for long term school adjustment and success, particularly as kindergarten teacher-child relationships have been found to predict sixth grade school social competence (Hamre & Pianta, 2001).

For all children, positive relationships with peers as well as teachers are important as children begin formal schooling. Children who start school with difficult peer interactions (e.g., aggressive behavior, exclusion from peer interactions) tend to be distracted from the main task of learning in school, often disrupting the learning of other children (Howes & Ritchie, 2002). These difficult children are at risk for forming conflictual relationships with their teachers. Teachers may be struggling not only with these children's behavior, but also a disrupted classroom (Howes & Shiver, 2006). Poor relationships with peers early in children's school careers can also interfere with later successful school adjustment (Ladd & Troop-Gordon, 2003). Despite a relatively large body of work documenting the negative association between poor social skills and school success, there is relatively little literature examining the antecedents of peer-related school readiness skills.

The second purpose of this research was to examine the association between home and child care antecedents of children's social relationships in pre-kindergarten. Adult-child dyadic relationships (e.g., child care providers, teachers, mothers) may differ widely in terms of emotional intensity and behavioral style (Howes, 1999). There is some controversy in the literature that examines child care antecedents of socially competent behaviors in school. One body of literature finds that teachers can perceive some children as less socially competent in kindergarten when they have attended child care (National Institute of Child Health and Human Development [NICHD] Early Child Care Research Network [ECCRN], 2003). One explanation for the negative associations between child care and social competence in formal school is that mothers who are less sensitive in their interactions with their children select child care settings with teachers who are also less positive in their interactions with the children; mothers who are more sensitive in their interactions with their children select more positive child care experiences for their child (NICHD ECCRN, 1997). Another body of literature suggests that there is continuity between child care and formal school (Howes, Hamilton, & Phillipsen, 1998). For example, children who establish close and non-conflictual relationships with their child care providers prior to formal school entry are likely to have positive kindergarten teacher-child relationships (Howes, Phillipsen, & Peisner-Feinberg, 2000).

In this paper we examine the association between maternal emotional availability and children's child care experiences at age 3 with children's social competence in pre-kindergarten. Based on previous research we anticipated that early experiences at home and in child care would be related to social competence in pre-kindergarten. However, Mexican-heritage children may experience differences in parenting styles that differentially influence the relation between emotional availability, child care at age 3, and their later social competence.

Due to the variation in the research findings on interactions among maternal emotional availability, maternal child care use for 3-year-old children, and children's social competence in pre-kindergarten, we explored several different hypotheses in this study. The first hypothesis concerns the potential negative influence of child care attendance on pre-kindergarten social competence. Therefore, we tested whether children enrolled in child care at age 3 were less socially competent in pre-kindergarten than children who were not enrolled in child care. The second hypothesis concerns differences in mothers who enroll their children in child care. Therefore, we tested whether children enrolled in child care at age 3 were different in emotional availability scores at age 3 from children not enrolled in child care. The third set of hypotheses concerns the potential interactions between experiences at home and experiences in child care in predicting social competence at pre-kindergarten, generally, and more specifically the interaction between maternal sensitivity and child care attendance. To examine these hypotheses we examined associations between experiences with mothers and child care providers, and the joint predictability of home and child care experiences for pre-kindergarten social competence.

Method

Participants

Fifty-three children and their mothers participated in this research. These participants were a subset of a larger national longitudinal evaluation of Early Head Start (Love et al., 2005). At the time of the child's birth all of the mothers agreed to participate in the National Early Head Start Evaluation and were randomly assigned to one local intervention group. The local intervention involved weekly home visits until the child was 3-years-old. The current sample used in this analysis was limited to mothers who self-identified as Mexican-heritage women, participated in data collection when the children were within 2 months of their third birthday, and enrolled their children in a pre-kindergarten program in the academic year prior to entering kindergarten. Twenty-three of the 53 children were girls. Seventy-four percent had a sibling.

All of the mothers spoke Spanish (95% only Spanish) and all of the mothers and children used Spanish as the household language. Only 15% of the mothers had documents that permitted them to legally work and live in the United States. Eighty-two percent of the mothers were not born in the United States. These mothers tended to be migrant workers who had come from rural areas around Oaxaca and Jalisco, Mexico, as young women, on the average 3.1 years prior to the birth of the target child. The mothers ranged in age from 14 to 35 years when their child was born, with an average maternal age of 26.2 years ($SD = 6.12$). Mothers had an average of 9 years of education ($SD = 3.75$) at the time of the children's pre-kindergarten assessment.

At 36 months, 37 children (69.8%) were enrolled in child care. More than three-quarters (77%) of these enrolled children were in center-based care. Almost all (92%) of the children enrolled in child care had Latino providers, spoke Spanish with their providers (83%) and with their peers (84%). When children were enrolled in center-based care they were in age-graded classrooms with an average of 8.3 children per adult and 18.3 children per classroom. The six children in family child care homes were in mixed age groups with an average of 7.3 children per adult and 9.32 children per family child care home.

All of the children were enrolled in public full- or half-day, center-based pre-K programs sponsored by the California Department of Education. These programs included only children who would be age-appropriate for kindergarten in the subsequent school year. The programs were on the campus of the neighborhood elementary school and had an average of 20.8 children per classroom. Each classroom had two teachers, 58% of the teachers had BA degrees in child development or a related field, and the remaining teachers had AA degrees in child development or a related field. We used the Early Childhood Environmental Rating Scale (ECERS; Harms, Clifford, & Cryer, 1998) to assess the quality of the classrooms. No classroom received a score of less than 3 indicating poor care and 84% of the classrooms received scores of 5 or higher indicating good care. The average ECERS score was 5.89.

Procedures

The data collected in this study were collected in Spanish by research assistants who were bilingual in Spanish and English, and were of Mexican or Central American descent. The research assistants were recruited through advertisements in local newspapers. All of the research assistants were blind with regard to the hypotheses of the study. All interviews were conducted in an open-ended conversational style rather than by administering formal instruments. Interviews were recorded, transcribed, and translated with English and Spanish versions available to raters and coders. When predetermined codes were utilized during naturalistic observation, the code sheets were in English. Field notes were written in a combination of the two languages. All raters of videotapes and field notes were bilingual in Spanish and English.

All mothers were visited in their homes to be observed and interviewed when the children were within 2 months of their third birthday. The entire visit lasted 2 to 3 hours and included participant observation (e.g., going to the store or park with the mother and child; being offered and accepting a small meal), as well as naturalistic observation and video-taping of ongoing interaction. The coded mother-child interaction used in this analysis came from a videotape of the last 30 minutes of the home visit. The first 25 minutes of the video-taping recorded on-going interaction. The last 5 minutes of the video-tape was more structured. The visitor handed the mother a dog hand puppet and asked her to play with the child with the puppet.

Thirty-seven of the children were visited in their regular child care arrangement within 2 months of their third birthday. The other 16 children were not enrolled in child care and were therefore only observed at home. We used naturalistic time-sample observations to collect data in the child care setting. During the naturalistic time-sampling, the observer recorded observations every 20 seconds for 5 minutes on predetermined code sheets (e.g., complex social pretend play; adult scaffolds child play with toy). There were 3, 5-minute time-sampled observations during each visit. These observations took place at the midpoint of the visit, and then twice during the second half of the visit, creating a total of 15 minutes of coded naturalistic observations per child. This resulted in 45 observations for each behavior.

All of the children were visited in their pre-kindergarten programs at the end of the academic year just prior to enrolling in kindergarten. We used the same naturalistic time-sample observational procedure except that four, not three, observations were collected. We also used the Child Behavior Ratings (CBR) scale (Ladd, 1999) to rate the content of peer interaction. These ratings were made four times for each child over the day of the Pre-K visit, occurring after each 5-minute naturalistic observation.

All research assistants were trained by one of the authors. In all cases, training consisted of intensive instruction with video records of mothers and children and then field training in homes and preschools. Following training, each observer reached at least 85% agreement with the trainer on each item of each measure. Inter-observer reliability checks between pairs of observers were conducted on home visits to children not in the research sample throughout the several years of data collection. The median weighted Kappas for observational measures used in this analysis are included in the description of each measure.

Measures

Emotional Availability Scale

The videotapes made at the home visit were coded using the Emotional Availability Scale (EAS), Second Edition: Infancy to Early Childhood Version (Biringen, Matheny, Bretherton, Renouf, & Sherman, 2000). The EAS has the following five subscales: (a) maternal sensitivity, (b) maternal structuring, (c) maternal overt and covert hostility, (d) child emotional responsiveness, and (e) involvement with mother (Biringen et al., 2000). Maternal sensitivity (e.g., attentive listening, comforting and playful physical contact) toward her child is rated on a 9-point scale, with higher scores indicating more sensitivity. Maternal structuring (e.g., actively engaging the child without being intrusive) is rated on a 7-point continuum with a score of 7 indicating optimal structuring. Maternal hostility (e.g., harsh or frightening words or actions) is rated on a 5-point scale with a score of 1 indicating low levels of hostility. Children's responsiveness (e.g., children respond in a positive manner to adult social bids) and involvement (e.g., children engage in the activity, are not anxious or avoiding) are rated on 7-point scales with a score of 5 indicating moderately optimal scores on both subscales. Children's responsiveness to the parent refers to their exploration and mastery of the world using the parent as a secure base, and responding to the parent with genuine appropriate affect. Children's involvement with the mother assesses the ability of the child to invite the adult into play. Maternal and child EAS scores predict social competence in pre-kindergarten (Biringen et al., 2005). One score per subscale was assigned. The rater, of Guatemalan heritage, was trained to inter-rater reliability using the weighted Kappa statistic (exact agreement; criterion of K_w = .70) prior to coding the videotapes. The rater assigned scores to the last section of the video only after watching the home-based mother child interaction in it's entirety to take into account the overall interaction style of the mother and the child.

Form of Care

Based on the descriptive field notes written by the observer, each child's child care type was coded for the type of care observed. Examples of these categories included: care by the father with the mother absent, care by another relative, or formal child care (either family child care or center-based care). Only two children were cared for by their fathers and one by a relative. The other children were all cared for in licensed family child care homes or child care centers.

Language and Ethnicity in Child Care

Based on conversations with the provider, the observers who conducted the child care visits recorded the ethnicity of the child care provider as either Latina or not. Children with Latina child care providers were then coded as having an ethnically matched provider. The observers also recorded the predominant language used in interaction by adults and children in the child care environment as English or Spanish. Predominant was coded as at least 60% of the interactions. Children were then coded as having (or not) their home language used with adults and with peers in child care.

Behavioral Observations of Children's Experiences with Child Care Providers

The following behaviors were coded as present or absent during the 45, 20-second interval naturalistic observations of child care settings: (a) caregiver language use with child, (b) joint attention with caregiver, and (c) adult scaffold of child play with toy. To better understand the frequency of each behavior within an observation period, a proportion of the overall observation time that the behavior was observed was calculated, which is a common procedure for analyzing data from behavioral observations (Bakeman & Dabbs, 1976). The number of times that a code was marked as present for a given interval of observation time was totaled and an average was calculated between the number of observation intervals in which the targeted behavior was observed and the total number of observation intervals. For example, if 10 of the 20-second observation intervals were coded as "joint attention with caregiver," then, the proportion would be 10 divided by 45, or a proportion of 0.22.

The "child care provider language use with child" score was created through summing the proportion of the observation period that the provider spent expanding the child's vocalizations into words, phrases, or sentences $(K = .79)$; engaging the child in conversation $(K = .81)$; and reading to the child $(K = .81)$. "Joint attention with child care provider" $(K = .83)$ was coded when the child care provider and child were attending to the same object. Either one could be looking at or touching the object, or if one was talking about (but not looking at or touching) the object and the other was touching or looking at the object. Finally, "child care provider scaffold of child play with toy" $(K = .86)$ was coded when the provider gave the child a toy, pointed out a feature of the toy, labeled the toy or talked about a toy, or taught the child something about the toy and/or its use. Similar behavioral observations of children's interactions with child care providers predict children's concurrent social competence (Kontos, Howes, Galinsky, & Shinn, 1997; Kontos & Keyes, 1999).

Adult Involvement Scale

The Adult Involvement Scale was included in the naturalistic observations in child care settings (Howes & Stewart, 1987). The appropriate code was recorded every 20 seconds during the naturalistic observations. The scale has six levels: (a) ignoring the child; (b) routine caregiving in which the provider does not socially engage the child (e.g., blowing nose); (c) minimal caregiving when the provider talks to or touches the child in order to discipline the child, to answer direct requests for help, or to give verbal directives; (d) answering the child's social bids in a positive but brief manner; (e) extending and elaborating the child's social bids, and, finally, (f) intense caregiving defined as entering into the child's activities as a mutual and reciprocating participant (e.g., a game of "peek-a-boo"). Low-level involvement is considered routine and minimal. High-level involvement is defined as extended and intense. Percent of responsive involvement ($K = .86$) was the percentage of the observation in which the child is within 3 feet of the adult and the adult involvement is simple responsive, elaborative, or intense (scale points 4, 5, or 6). The Adult Involvement Scale has been used in many large scale studies of children's child care experiences where it has been used to predict children's concurrent social competence (Burchinal & Cryer, 2003).

Revised Peer Play Scale

Engagement with peers and the structural complexity of that play with peers including pretend play in pre-kindergarten was measured using the Revised Peer Play Scale (Howes & Matheson, 1992). This scale was normed on a longitudinal sample of children attending center-based child care (Howes & Matheson, 1992). The ethnic composition of the norming sample was 61% European American, 22% Latino, 14% African American, and 2% Asian American. It was subsequently validated in several multi-ethnic samples (Howes & Lee, 2004), including a rural Mexican sample (Farver & Howes, 1993).

During the naturalistic time-sampling, coding was conducted using the Revised Peer Play Scale. The Revised Peer Play Scale has six scale points. The first scale points measure low-level peer play (ranging from "solitary" to "parallel" play), and were therefore not used in our analysis. The remaining scale points capture interactive peer play and range from "parallel-aware" to "cooperative pretend play." We defined engaging with peers as the proportion of the observation period that peer play was coded as at least parallel play with eye contact ($K = .95$). That is, the target child and the peer were playing with similar objects or in similar ways and exchanged eye glances as they played.

Our measure of structurally complex peer interaction was defined through the norming and validation of the Revised Peer Play Scale (Howes & Matheson, 1992). In this work, complementary/reciprocal play emerged as a competent play form before 13 to 15 months, cooperative social pretend play as a competent play form before 30 to 35 months, and complex social pretend play as a competent play form before 42 to 48 months.

Complementary/reciprocal play ($K = .86$) was defined as instances when children were playing with each other and one child's play behavior followed the other and there was "role reversal." Role reversal means that each child not only knows what he/she is doing in the game but also what the other child is doing and they can play either role. There are at least two roles in the play and each child takes turns playing at both roles in their "script." For example, playing hide and seek, where one child is the hider while the other child is the seeker. After the hider is found, the children can reverse the roles.

Cooperative pretend play ($K = .93$) was play that occurred between two or more children and involved pretense, make believe or fantasy, or projecting an imaginary situation onto an actual one, as in "make believe" play. Cooperative pretend play could involve (a) behavior (pretending to be asleep), (b) substitute objects (pretending a cloth is a pillow), or (c) imagining objects (pretending there is a pillow where there is no object). These are the more rudimentary forms of pretend play because the "script" is very straightforward. It only requires that an imaginary situation has been agreed upon by the target child and at least one other child. Cooperative pretend play can also involve imagined roles and situations, such as pretending to be a doctor or members of a family, wash dishes or cook supper, drive to the movies, or pretend to be a bear.

Complex pretend play ($K = .95$) was coded if the child and at least one peer were engaged in "cooperative pretend" play plus at least one of the following: (a) name roles ("I'm the doctor"), (b) explicitly assign roles ("You be the sister"), (c) go out of the role to modify the script ("The car hit you, but don't die"), (d) make a proposal to play pretend ("Let's pretend it's snowing and we're out in the cold"), (e) prompt the other ("Talk in a baby voice"), or (f) make it explicit in other ways that they are engaged in pretend play.

The measure of complex peer play used in this analysis was the proportion of the total time engaged with peers that the target child engaged in complementary-reciprocal play or cooperative pretend play or complex pretend. Pretend play was also calculated as the proportion of the observation period spent in pretend play (cooperative or complex).

Children's Behavior Ratings

The Child Behavior Ratings Scale (CBR) (Ladd, Birch, & Buhs, 1999; Ladd & Profilet, 1996) was used to rate the content of children's behavior with peers. In previous research these observer ratings predicted children's kindergarten school adjustment (Ladd et al., 1999). Observers made nine ratings with the CBR. The ratings were for: aggression towards peers, exclusion from peer activity, withdrawn/asocial behavior, anxious/fearful behavior, victim of aggression, pro-social with peers, sociability with peers, domineering with peers, and distractible behavior. A score of 5 reflects that the category was very characteristic of the child, a score of 3 indicates that the category was somewhat characteristic of the child, and a score of 1 means that the category was not very characteristic of the child during the observation.

Since we were using the CBR with a younger sample than Ladd and Profilet (1996), we used a principal components factor analysis with varimax rotation (accounting for 70% of the variance) to reduce the CBR nine peer ratings to three composite ratings of the child's observed behaviors with peers on the larger national sample ($N = 1180$). The three composites were aggressive with peers ($\alpha = .89$; $K = .87$), sociable with peers ($\alpha = .82$; $K = .85$), and excluded from peer play ratings ($\alpha = .82$; $K = .81$). The composite variable "aggressive with peers" consisted of two ratings: aggressive and domineering. The composite variable "sociable with peers" consisted of four ratings: prosocial, outgoing, withdrawn (reverse coded), and unoccupied (reverse coded). The composite variable "excluded from peer play" consisted of three ratings: excluded, victim, and anxious ratings. The composite scores were averaged across the four rating periods to provide one score for each child.

Student Teacher Relationship Scale

Pre-K teachers completed the Student Teacher Relationship Scale (STRS; Pianta, 2001), a widely-used 21-item scale assessing teacher perceptions of the quality of their relationships with specific students that yields *closeness* and *conflict* scores. Scores can range from 1 to 5, with 5 indicating higher ratings. The STRS has shown validity with regard to predicting academic and social functioning in Pre-K through the elementary grades (Hamre & Pianta, 2001; Pianta, Hamre, & Stuhlman, 2002). In prior work with large samples, the closeness and conflict scores had acceptable reliability (closeness: $\alpha = .87$; conflict: $\alpha = .92$; Hamre & Pianta, 2001; Pianta et al., 2002).

Caregiver's Child Report Form

We used the Caregiver's Child Report Form developed for the Head Start Family and Child Experiences Study (Tarullo, 2003) to assess teacher perceptions of children's behavior in preschool, Head Start, and pre-kindergarten classrooms. The first portion of the questionnaire consisted of 12 items, each assessing the frequency with which the child engaged in friendly, cooperative, and compliant behavior in class on a 3-point scale. These items were modified from Elliot et al.'s Social Skills Rating Scale (Elliot, Gresham, Freeman, & McCloskey, 1988). The second portion of the questionnaire consisted of 14 items each assessing the frequency with which the child engaged in aggressive, hyperactive, or depressed-withdrawn behavior in class during the past month, again using a 3-point scale. These items were adapted from the Child Behavior Checklist for Children (Alexander & Entwisle, 1989). In the current study, we used the first 12 items for social skills to create a social skills score ($\alpha = .90$). We used the 14 classroom conduct items from the second portion of the questionnaire to create a behavior problems score ($\alpha = .81$). This measure has had acceptable validity with regard to observed behavior (Tarullo, 2003).

Results

Overview

The results section is organized first with a description of participants and their behaviors at the child's third birthday and again when the child was in pre-kindergarten. Then analyses are presented, with simple associations and then hierarchical regression. The association between EAS scores at home when the child was 3-years-old and behaviors and ratings of social competence in pre-kindergarten were examined. Subsequently, interactions among social competence, emotional availability, enrollment in child care and maternal sensitivity in relation to children's behavior in pre-kindergarten were considered. Finally, we examined the additive predictability of EAS scores and observed behavior in child care for pre-kindergarten behavior.

Mothers, Child Care Providers, and Children at the Third Birthday

The mothers tended to receive high scores on the sensitivity subscale of the EAS. No mother scored lower than 6 on a 9-point scale. Mothers also received low scores on the hostility subscale. No mother scored higher than a 2 on a 5-point scale. Maternal structuring subscale scores tended to be at the scale midpoint, relatively lower than the sensitivity scores. Children scored at the high end on both the responsive and involvement subscales. See Table 1 for descriptive statistics and ranges.

Child care providers were responsively involved with children almost half of the time. Child care providers engaged in joint attention with the children 27% of the time and in language activity 20% of the time. Scaffolding children's play by providers was relatively infrequent, occurring only 8% of the time. See Table 2 for descriptive statistics and ranges.

Children's Social Competence in Pre-Kindergarten

Children spent relatively little time in complex peer play or social pretend play in pre-kindergarten. They also tended to be rated as sociable rather than aggressive or excluded in their peer interactions. Pre-K teachers rated the children as relatively high in close relationships and social skills and relatively low in conflict relationships or problem behaviors. See Table 3 for descriptive statistics and ranges.

Table 1
Emotional Availability Scores

EAS Subscale	M	SD	Range
Maternal			
Sensitivity[a]	7.14	.58	6 - 8
Hostility[b]	1.11	.32	1 - 2
Structure[c]	4.74	.55	3 - 5
Child			
Responsive[c]	6.40	1.29	3 - 7
Involvement[c]	6.45	1.12	3 - 7

Note. n = 53.
[a]Possible score range = 1 - 9. [b]Possible score range = 1 - 5. [c]Possible score range = 1 - 7.

Table 2
Proportion of Child Care Observation Spent in Interaction with Child Care Provider

	M	*SD*	Range
Behavior observations			
Child care provider language use with child	.20	.31	.00 - 1.00
Joint attention with child care provider	.27	.26	.02 - .87
Child care provider scaffolds child play with toy	.08	.10	.00 - .30
Adult involvement scale			
Responsive Involvement	.40	.27	.06 - .91

Note. n = 37.

Associations Between Maternal and Child Emotional Availability at Age Three and Pre-Kindergarten Social Competence

Children's complex peer play in pre-kindergarten was associated with maternal structuring and child involvement as 3-year-olds, but not with maternal sensitivity. Children's pretend play with peers in pre-kindergarten was associated with maternal sensitivity and structuring and with child involvement as 3-year-olds. Children's exclusion by peers in pre-kindergarten was negatively associated with child involvement with mother as 3-year-olds. There were no significant associations between emotional availability at three years and pre-kindergarten relationships with teachers. See Table 4 for Pearson product-moment correlations.

Table 3
Social Competence in Pre-Kindergarten

	M	SD	Range
Revised Peer Play Scale[a]			
Complex play	.13	.14	.00 - .55
Pretend	.04	.09	.00 - .45
Children's Behavior Ratings[b]			
Sociable	3.95	.97	1 - 5
Aggressive	1.45	.40	1 - 5
Excluded	1.25	.53	1 - 5
Student Teacher Relationship[b]			
Close relationship	3.34	.85	1 - 5
Conflict relationships	1.50	.67	1 - 5
Caregiver's Child Report Form[c]			
Social skills	2.49	.36	1 - 3
Behavior problems	1.33	.32	1 - 3

Note. n = 53.
[a]Possible range = 0.0 - 1.00. [b]Possible range = 1 - 5. [c]Possible range = 1 - 3.

Differences among mothers and children who did and did not use child care at 36 months

Emotional availability scores. We used a multivariate analysis of covariance, controlling for gender, sibling status, and maternal education to compare EAS scores for mothers and children who did and did not use child care at 36 months. There were no significant differences between groups, $F(5, 47) = 1.10, p = .37$. See Table 5 for marginal means for these comparisons.

Pre-kindergarten social competence. We used a multivariate analysis of covariance, controlling for gender, sibling status, and maternal education to compare pre-kindergarten social competence scores for children who did and did not use child care at 36 months. There were no significant differences between groups, $F(9, 34) = .50, p = .87$. See Table 5 for marginal means for these comparisons.

Associations Between Emotional Availability at Home and Child Care Experiences When Children were 3-years-old

We examined associations between maternal and child emotional availability, and children's experiences with child care providers using Pearson product-moment correlations. There were no significant associations (all r values < .04).

Table 4

Pearson Correlations Between maternal and Child Emotional Availability and Social Competence in Pre-kindergarten

| | Emotional availability at age three | | | | |
	Sensitivity	Hostility	Structure	Responsive	Involvement
Pre-kindergarten measures					
Revised Peer Play Scale					
Complex play	.19	-.01	.27*	-.09	.27*
Pretend	.34**	-.05	.28*	-.14	.35**
Children's Behavior Ratings					
Sociable	.19	.04	.20	.15	.15
Aggresive	-.09	.12	.19	.05	-.09
Excluded	-.05	.09	-.12	-.19	-.32*
Student Teacher Relationship					
Close	.13	-.03	-.05	.11	.05
Conflict	-.24	.07	-.12	.00	-.03
Caregiver's Child Report Form					
Social skills	.24	-.07	.02	.04	.02
Behavior problems	-.18	.07	-.03	-.06	-.11

Note. n = 53. *$p \leq .05$; ** $p \leq .01$.

Table 5

Comparisons of Behaviors Based on Child Care Enrollment at Age 3

	Enrolled in Child Care	
	No	Yes
Emotional Availability at age 3		
Mothers		
Sensitivity	6.99	7.21
Structure	4.73	4.74
Hostility	1.11	1.12
Child		
Involvement	6.31	6.31
Responsive	6.83	6.21
Pre-kindergarten Social Competence		
Revised Peer Play Scale		
Complex Play	.12	.13
Pretend	.04	.04
Children's Behavior Ratings		
Sociable	4.11	4.16
Aggressive	1.22	1.23
Excluded	1.83	1.21
Pre-kindergarten social competence		
Student Teacher Relationship		
Close	4.48	4.44
Conflict	1.16	1.14
Caregiver Child Report Form		
Social Skills	2.49	2.48
Behavior Problems	1.34	1.29

Note: Numbers in table are marginal means controlling for gender, sibling status, and maternal education.

Predicting Social Competence at Pre-Kindergarten: Does Early Maternal Sensitivity Mediate Early Child Care Use?

Through a hierarchical linear regression analysis we examined the hypothesis that less sensitive mothers who use child care would have less competent children in pre-kindergarten. We entered the maternal or child emotional availability subscale score most highly correlated with the pre-kindergarten outcome as a first step. We then entered child care use at age three as a second step, we entered the interaction of child care use and maternal sensitivity as a test of the mediational effect. This analysis is presented in Table 6. The mediational hypothesis was only supported for one outcome: complex play with peers. Mothers who were relatively less sensitive and used child care tended to have children who engaged in less complex play with peers. Consistent with the simple correlational analysis, children with higher involvement scores at age 3 engaged in more pretend play and were less likely to be excluded by peers in pre-kindergarten.

Table 6
Predicting Social Competence in Pre-kindergarten

Predictor	R	R^2	$R^2 \Delta$	Final β
Revised Peer Play Scale				
Complex play				
Structure	.35*	.13		.21
Involvement				.25
Child care use	.40*	.16	.03	1.89*
Interaction: Sensitivity and Child Care	.47*	.22	.06*	-1.73*
Pretend				
Sensitivity	.49*	.24		.30
Involvement				.36*
Child care use	.50*	.25	.01	.52
Interaction: Sensitivity and Child Care	.50*	.25	.00	.45
Children's Behavior Ratings				
Excluded				
Involvement	.32*	.10		-.34*
Child care use	.34*	.12	.02	.02
Interaction: Sensitivity and Child Care	.34	.12	.00	.12

Note: $*p \leq .05; ***p \leq .01$.

Associations Between Children's Experiences in Child Care and Pre-Kindergarten Social Competence

 Finally, for the subsample of children enrolled in child care at age 3 we examined associations between their experiences in child care at age 3 and their pre-kindergarten social competence. These Pearson product-moment correlations are in Table 7. Children's earlier joint attention and scaffolding experiences with child care providers were associated with their later pre-kindergarten complex play and pretend play with peers. Child care providers' responsive involvement with children at age 3 was positively associated with their pretend play and negatively associated with their exclusion ratings.

 Child care provider scaffolding of children when they were 3-years-old was positively associated with their pre-kindergarten teachers' ratings of their social skills in pre-kindergarten and negatively associated with their aggression with peers, conflictual relationships with teachers, and teacher ratings of behavior problems in pre-kindergarten.

 We used hierarchical regression analysis to examine whether for children enrolled in child care (n = 37), their child care experiences added to the predictability of maternal and child emotional availability[1].

 We first entered the emotional availability subscale score with the highest simple correlation with the outcome and then as a subsequent step entered the child care experience variable with the highest simple correlation. In only one outcome, complex play with peers, was the maternal emotional availability score still significant after entering the child care experiences.

 Complex play with peers was significantly predicted by child involvement (β= .42, p = .02) and child care provider scaffolding (β = .38, p = .03) (R = .72, R^2 = .52, p = .001). Consistent with the correlational analysis, pretend play could be predicted by child care provider joint attention (β = .51, p = .01) (R = .59, R^2 = .34, p = .005). Being excluded could be negatively predicted by child care provider responsive involvement (β = .4, p = .05) (R = .36, R^2 = .14, p = .05). Conflictual teacher-child relationships could be negatively predicted by child care provider scaffolding (β = -.41, p = .05) (R = .41, R^2 = .17, p = .05). Social skills could be positively predicted (β = .41, p = .05) (R = .43, R^2 = .19, p = .05) and problem behaviors (β = -.44, p = .05) (R = .43, R^2 = .19, p = .05) negatively predicted by child care provider scaffolding.

---

[1] Given the small sample size only 2 predictors were used for each outcome.

Table 7
Pearson Correlations Between Child Care Experiences and Social Competence in Pre-kindergarten

| | Child Care Experiences | | | |
	Language	Joint attention	Scaffolding	Responsive
Revised Peer Play Scale				
Complex play	.10	.35*	.42**	.17
Pretend	.00	.55**	.40**	.36*
Children's Behavior Ratings				
Sociable	.13	.25	.12	.16
Aggressive	.03	.02	-.27*	.07
Excluded	-.13	-.08	-.01	-.31*
Student Teacher Relationship				
Close	.07	.01	.25	.24
Conflict	.10	.14	-.27*	.02
Caregiver Report Form				
Social skills	.05	.07	.43*	.10
Behavior problems	-.06	-.20	-.42*	-.03

Note. $n = 37$. $p \le .05$; ** $p \le .01$.

To directly examine our expectation that maternal and child care provider scaffolding would predict pre-kindergarten social competence, we used a second set of hierarchical regressions. In these regressions the emotional availability structuring score was entered first and then the child care provider scaffolding score. Complex play with peers (β maternal $= .34$, $p = .05$; β child care $= .41$, $p = .05$) ($R = .54$, $R^2 = .24$, $p = .01$), pretend play with peers (β maternal $= .49$, $p = .05$; β child care $= .38$, $p = .05$) ($R = .63$, $R^2 = .35$, $p = .01$), social skills (β maternal $= .04$, n.s.; β child care $= .42$, $p = .03$) ($R = .43$, $R^2 = .18$, $p = .05$), and problem behaviors (β maternal $= -.11$, *n.s.*; β child care $= -.41$, $p = .04$) ($R = .43$, $R^2 = .19$, $p = .05$) could be significantly predicted.

Discussion

Consistent with our expectations, Mexican heritage children's experiences with structure and scaffolding in their adult-child interactions at home and at child care were positively associated with later observed and rated social competence with teachers and peers in pre-kindergarten. These findings must be tempered by the very high overall sensitivity ratings of the mothers. We suspect that structuring along with a high base level of sensitivity accounts for these findings. Mothers who were rated as emotionally available, *and* who provided a structure for their children to interpret social and learning experiences, better prepared their children for the social-competence demands of dominant culture early schooling.

Children with and without child care experience were no different in their experiences of emotional availability at home or in their social competence as pre-kindergarteners. However, not all child care experiences were the same. Scaffolding of interactions with materials was associated with social competence in pre-kindergarten. Thus, this study replicated earlier studies of dominant culture families that suggest the roots of social competence in school are to be found within experiences both at home and in child care (Howes et al., 1998; Thompson & Raikes, 2003).

Again, consistent with prior research (NICHD ECCRN, 1997), when mothers had lower EAS sensitivity ratings and used child care, their children experienced some difficulty in constructing play with peers in pre-kindergarten. Again, this conclusion must be tempered by the relatively high overall sensitivity ratings. Since no mother was rated as insensitive (the bottom of the sensitivity scale), it was only when relatively less sensitive mothers used child care that we found an association. It appears that relatively less sensitive mothers were less likely to select child care experiences that enhanced children's play with peers. There is some indication in the literature to suggest that Latina mothers and child care providers may not see themselves as instrumental in shaping children's encounters with peers (Howes, Wishard Guerra, & Zucker, 2008). Thus it is unlikely these mothers selected child care on the basis of opportunities to play with peers. However, children coming from homes and child care programs where adults do not help children to negotiate peer play may be at a disadvantage in schools that encourage peer collaboration as part of the curriculum of academic learning.

One of the limitations of this study is the small sample size with little variability in overall high maternal sensitivity. More predictive relations may have been found in a larger more heterogeneous sample. However, the sensitivity of these Latina mothers may be seen as a strength of this sample. This high level of sensitivity may provide emotional security, helping children to be prepared for new challenges, including school.

Future interventions might directly target Latina mothers, encouraging Latina mothers to build from their base of sensitivity to their children, using their sensitive ways of responding to enhance their teaching/scaffolding/structuring at home in order to build a link between home and school. For example, kindergarten transition and/or child care programs could hold parent-child workshops where parents could be guided in helping their child with a project. This might also help these Latina mothers to be more knowledgeable about the American schooling system and the increasing expectations that parents be involved in their child's learning (e.g., helping with homework). It might also be possible to use the EAS as a teaching tool as well as an evaluation tool because it includes both the dimensions of sensitivity and structuring in a manner that provides a scaffold rather than a control.

The Emotional Availability Scale was developed with dominant culture families. Our findings point to the strength of this measure because it was also able to capture significant dimensions of behavior in Mexican-heritage families. In particular our findings underscore the importance of measuring both maternal sensitivity and structuring. Our findings further suggest that it would be advantageous to use the EAS with child care providers and teachers as well as parents in future research protocols.

In summary, the children of Mexican-heritage mothers with higher ratings on the EAS maternal structuring and sensitivity scales appeared socially competent as they were about to enter kindergarten. Being enrolled in child care at age 3 was unrelated to the mother's and children's EAS scores but children of relatively less sensitive mothers who were enrolled in child care seem less competent with peers at pre-kindergarten. In addition, when children had more sensitive experiences in child care as well as at home, then children's providers in child care scaffolding of their activities was positively related to pre-kindergarten social competence.

References

Alexander, K. L., & Entwisle, D. R. (1989). Achievement in the first two years of school: Patterns and processes. *Monographs of the Society for Research in Child Development, 53*, 1-157

Bakeman, R., & Dabbs, J. (1976). Social interaction observed. *Personality and Social Psychology Bulletin, 2*, 335-345.

Biringen, Z., Matheny, A., Bretherton, I., Renouf, A., & Sherman, M. (2000). Maternal representations of the self as parent: Connections with maternal sensitivity and maternal structuring. *Attachment and Human Development, 2*, 218-232.

Biringen, Z., Skillern, S., Mone, J., & Pianta, R. (2005). Emotional availability is predictive of the emotional aspects of children's "school readiness." *Journal of Early Childhood and Infant Psychology, 1*, 19-32.

Burchinal, M., & Cryer, D. (2003). Diversity, child care quality, and developmental outcomes. *Early Childhood Research Quarterly, 18*, 401-426.

Easterbrooks, M. A., & Biringen, Z. (2000). Guest editors' introduction to the special issue: Mapping the terrain of emotional availability and attachment.

Attachment and Human Development, 2, 123-129.

Elliot, S. N., Gresham, F., Freeman, R., & McCloskey, G. (1988). Teacher and observer ratings of children's social skills: Validation of the Social Skills Rating Scales. *Journal of Psychoeducational Assessment, 6*, 152-161.

Farver, J. M., & Howes, C. (1993). Cultural differences in American and Mexican mother-child pretend play. *Merrill Palmer Quarterly, 30*, 344-358.

Farver, J. M., Xu, Y., Eppe, S., & Lonigan, C. (2006). Home environments and young Latino children's school readiness. *Early Childhood Research Quarterly, 21*, 196-212.

Halgunseth, L. C., Ispa, J., & Rudy, D. D. (2006). Parental control in Latino families: An integrative review. *Child Development, 77*, 1282-1297.

Hamre, B., & Pianta, R. C. (2001). Early teacher-child relationships and trajectory of school outcomes through eighth grade. *Child Development, 72*, 625-638.

Hamre, B., & Pianta, R. C. (2005). Can instructional and emotional support in the first grade classroom make a difference for children at risk for school failure? *Child Development, 76*, 949-967.

Harms, T., Clifford, R. M., & Cryer, D. (1998). *Early Childhood Environment Rating Scale: Revised edition*. New York: Teachers College Press.

Howes, C. (1999). Attachment relationships in the context of multiple caregivers. In J. Cassidy & P. R. Shaver (Eds.), *Handbook of attachment theory and research* (pp. 671-687). New York: Guilford.

Howes, C., Hamilton, C. E., & Phillipsen, L. (1998). Stability and continuity of child-caregiver and child-peer relationships. *Child Development, 69*, 418-426.

Howes, C., & Lee, L. (2004). Peer relations in young children. In L. Balter & C. Tamis-LeMonda (Eds.), *Child psychology: A handbook of contemporary issues* (Vol. 2) (pp. 135-152). New York: Taylor & Francis.

Howes, C., & Matheson, C. C. (1992). Sequences in the development of competent play with peers social and social pretend play. *Developmental Psychology, 28*, 961-974.

Howes, C., Phillipsen, L., & Peisner-Feinberg, E. (2000). The consistency and predictability of teacher-child relationships during the transition to kindergarten. *Journal of School Psychology, 38*, 113-132.

Howes, C., & Ritchie, S. (2002). *A matter of trust: Connecting teachers and learners in the early childhood classroom*. New York: Teachers College Press.

Howes, C., & Shiver, E. M. (2006). New child-caregiver attachment relationships: Entering child care when the caregiver is and is not an ethnic match. *Social Development, 15*, 343-360.

Howes, C., & Stewart, P. (1987). Child's play with adults, toys, and peers: An examination of family and child-care influences. *Developmental Psychology, 23*, 423-430.

Howes, C., Wishard Guerra, A., & Zucker, E. (2008). Migrating from Mexico and sharing pretend with peers in the United States. *Merrill Palmer Quarterly,*

54, 256-288.

Kontos, S., Howes, C., Galinsky, E., & Shinn, M. B. (1997). Children's experiences in family child care and relative care as a function of family income and ethnicity. *Merrill Palmer Quarterly, 43*, 386-403.

Kontos, S., & Keyes, L. (1999). An ecobehavioral analysis of early childhood classrooms. *Early Childhood Research Quarterly, 14*, 35-50.

Ladd, G. W. (1999). Peer relationships and social competence during early and middle childhood. *American Review of Psychology, 50*, 333-359.

Ladd, G. W., Birch, S., & Buhs, E. S. (1999). Children's social and scholastic lives in kindergarten: Related spheres of influence. *Child Development, 70*, 1373-1400.

Ladd, G. W., & Profilet, S. M. (1996). The Child Behavior Scale: A teacher-report measure of young children's aggressive, withdrawn and prosocial behaviors. *Developmental Psychology, 32*, 1008-1024.

Ladd, G. W., & Troop-Gordon, W. (2003). The role of chronic peer difficulties in the problems of children's psychological adjustment. *Child Development, 74*, 1344-1367.

La Paro, K. M., & Pianta, R. C. (2000). Predicting children's competence in the early school years: A meta-analytic review. *Review of Educational Research, 70*, 443-484.

Love, J., Kisker, E. E., Ross, C., Raikes, H., Constantine, J., Boller, K., et al. (2005). The effectiveness of Early Head Start for 3-year-old children and their parents: Lessons for policy and programs. *Developmental Psychology, 41*, 885-901.

National Institute of Child Health and Human Development (NICHD) Early Child Care Research Network (ECCRN). (1997). The effects of infant child care on infant-mother attachment security: Results of the NICHD study of early child care. *Child Development, 68*, 860-879.

NICHD ECCRN. (2003). Does amount of time in child care predict socioemotional adjustment during the transition to kindergarten? *Child Development, 74*, 976-1005.

Pianta, R. C. (2001). *Student Teacher Relationship Scale.* Lutz, FL: Psychological Assessment Resources, Inc.

Pianta, R. C., Hamre, B., & Stuhlman, M. (Eds.). (2002). *Relationships between teachers and children* (Vol. 7). New York: Wiley.

Reese, L. (2002). Parental strategies in contrasting cultural settings: Families in Mexico and El Norte. *Anthropology and Education Quarterly, 33*, 30-59.

Tarullo, T. (2003, April). *A whole-child perspective on Head Start reform: Findings on children's cognitive and socio-emotional development from FACES 2000.* Paper presented at the Society for Research in Child Development, Tampa, FL.

Thompson, R. A., & Raikes, H. A. (2003). Towards the next quarter-century: Conceptual and methodological challenges for attachment theory. *Development and Psychopathology, 15*, 691-718.

Using the Emotional Availability Scales along the Child Care Continuum

Eva Marie Shivers
Institute for Child Development Research & Social
Change, Indigo Cultural Center

The use of the Emotional Availability Scales (EAS) with non-maternal caregivers was considered. The first section presents evidence on attachment relationships in child care to argue that extending the construct of emotional availability to child care providers is not only appropriate, but elemental in understanding the impact of early learning experiences on children's concurrent and future developmental outcomes. Findings from recent studies that have piloted the use of the EAS in various child care arrangements with diverse samples of children and caregivers are reviewed based on two different frameworks – an investment model and a family-support model. The paper concludes by discussing several practice and policy implications of using the EAS in child care research, and next steps in emotional availability and child care research.

Although previous studies on emotional availability involve parents and children, the authors of the Emotional Availability Scales (EAS) suggest that the use of these scales are also appropriate with non-parental caregivers. The authors of the EAS also encourage researchers to use the EAS to explore particular patterns of interactions with non-maternal caregivers (Easterbrooks & Biringen, 2000). Accordingly, extending the construct of emotional availability to child care providers is not only appropriate, but also elemental in understanding the impact of early learning experiences on children's concurrent and future developmental outcomes. The first objective of this paper is to explore the theoretical and conceptual underpinnings for using the EAS in settings along the child care continuum. The second section of this paper will review several child care studies in which emotional availability was a key construct. Last, implications for policy and practice will be discussed.

All correspondence should be addressed to Eva Marie Shivers, Institute for Child Development Research & Social Change, Indigo Cultural Center, 2942 North 24th Street, Suite 114-321, Phoenix, AZ 85016. Electronic mail may be sent to eshivers@indigoculturalcenter.com

Emotional Availability

The version of EAS discussed in this paper is the *Infancy and Early Childhood Version (3rd ed.)* of Biringen, Robinson, and Emde's (2000) *Emotional Availability Scales (EAS)*. This observational system captures emotional availability during caregiver-child interactions. The EAS adopt a relational coding approach. Within this approach, scoring of one dyadic member cannot be carried out independently of the other's actions. Thus, observers consider the behaviors of the other dyadic member when scoring either the provider's or the child's behavior. Dimensions of EAS of the child care provider include *caregiver sensitivity, caregiver structuring, caregiver non-intrusiveness, and caregiver non-hostility*. Dimensions of EAS for the child include *child responsiveness to the caregiver* and *child involvement of the caregiver in interaction*.

The EAS were developed to fill the need for a measure of maternal sensitivity that could be used in shorter observations than the more extensive observations used by Ainsworth, Blehar, Waters, and Wall (1978). Both measures are global scales of sensitivity focusing on behavioral style rather than discrete behaviors. The EAS extend Ainsworth's coding of maternal sensitivity and has specific behavioral descriptions of interactions. Ainsworth's global assessments rate maternal sensitivity-insensitivity, acceptance-rejection, cooperation-interference, and accessibility-ignoring. Each scale has 9 scale points, and 5 anchor points with detailed behavioral descriptions. Pearson product-moment correlations between the EAS and the Ainsworth et al. (1978) scale were over .90 in two samples (Biringen et al., 2000). Further, several studies have demonstrated concurrent validity with mother-child attachment security using the Strange Situation (Easterbrooks, Biesecker, & Lyons-Ruth, 2000; Easterbrooks & Biringen, 2000; Ziv, Aviezer, Gini, Sagi, & Koren-Karie, 2000).

Although attachment security and emotional availability have similar conceptual underpinnings, there are key distinctions between the two theories (Bretherton, 2000). Indeed, both constructs relate to the quality of caregiver-child interactions, but emotional availability has a slightly different theoretical lineage (Biringen & Robinson, 1991; Emde & Easterbrooks, 1985; Mahler, Pine, & Bergman, 1975). Emotional availability focuses more explicitly on emotion and affect attunement as a context for children's later emotional regulation (Easterbrooks et al., 2000) than attachment; indeed, when using the EAS, observers focus on evaluating how interactional missteps are repaired by the provider (Easterbrooks et al., 2000). Thus, the EAS were designed to capture not only how a caregiver responds, but also how caregivers provide their own emotional signals (Easterbrooks & Biringen, 2000). In addition to measuring caregiver sensitivity, the EAS also assess ways in which caregivers control children's behaviors (Easterbrooks & Biringen, 2005). Emotional availability explicitly acknowledges the child as an active contributor to the relationship, while this idea is more implicit in attachment constructs like *sensitivity* (Bretherton, 2000). In addition, although attachment theory places an emphasis on the role of caregiver sensitivity in conditions of stress or danger, emotional availability more broadly encompasses aspects of behavior that may not be pivotal to the role of the caregiver as the secure-base (Easterbrooks & Biringen, 2000). Regardless of the somewhat modest differences, an exploration of attachment theory is warranted because it is the most established theory developed regarding understanding children's emotional development in child care.

Attachment Theory and Provider-Child Relationships

There is congruence in the research literature on one essential element of quality child care settings: the presence of sensitive, nurturing providers who can build positive and trusting relationships with children (Howes, 1999; Lamb, 1998; National Institute of Child Health and Human Development [NICHD] Early Child Care Research Network [ECCRN], 1998; Shonkoff & Phillips, 2000; Wishard, Shivers, Howes, & Ritchie, 2003). Like much of the literature on parent-child emotional availability, a prevailing perspective on provider-child relationships in child care is drawn from attachment theory (Ainsworth et al., 1978; Bowlby, 1969/1982; Bretherton, 1985; Pianta, Steinberg, & Rollins, 1995). As such, this paper's key theoretical justification for extending the use of the EAS to child care settings is largely informed by attachment theory.

Attachment theory assumes that children use their relationships with significant adults to organize their experiences. Traditional research using attachment theory usually focuses on parents as attachment figures. So, when caregivers who are not the child's parents are included as attachment figures, standard criteria are necessary for their identification. Howes (1999) sets forth three criteria for the identification of children's attachment figures, they must (a) provide physical and emotional care, (b) contribute to continuity or consistency in the child's life, and (c) have an emotional investment in the child. Using these criteria, many child care studies operate on the assumption that child care providers qualify as attachment figures for the children in their care (Howes, 1999; Howes & Hamilton, 1993; Howes & Ritchie, 2002; Howes & Shivers, 2006; Pianta, Hamre, & Stuhlman, 2002; Wishard et al., 2003).

Using attachment theory as a framework, researchers have explored several notable trends in child care research. According to attachment theory (Bretherton, 1985) attachment relationships created between child care providers and young children will be based on the behavior repertoire that the adults and children bring to the relationship formation. Both adults and children draw on an established repertoire of behaviors based in part on prior relationship history and their home cultural community (Howes & Shivers, 2006). Children who have experienced positive attachment relationships at home are likely to enter child care trusting that they will be well cared for and be ready to establish new positive relationships (Howes & Ritchie, 2002; Mitchell-Copeland, Denham, & DeMulder, 1997; Mubler, Denham, Schmidt, & Mitchell, 2000). In contrast, children who have problematic relationships at home are likely to bring to child care behaviors (e.g., acting out, avoidance) that may lead to a less positive beginning.

Nevertheless, children do form attachment relationships with their caregivers that may be independent of parental attachment quality. Children with secure attachments to caregivers tend to be socially competent with peers and longitudinally have positive relationships with teachers (Howes, 1999; Mitchell-Copeland et al., 1997; Pianta et al., 2002). Also, the antecedents of attachment quality are similar for caregivers and parents. Caregivers who are rated as more sensitive in their interactions with children are associated with children's secure attachment scores (using the Attachment Q-Sort, Waters, 1990) (Howes, 1999).

Researchers have also used attachment theory as a framework for understanding how the quality of provider-child relationships impacts children's concurrent and future developmental outcomes. Optimal provider-child relationships are particularly important for children living in difficult life circumstances, such as poverty, as they may provide a buffer against negative developmental outcomes (Garmezy, 1993; McLoyd, 1990; Pedersen, Faucher & Eaton, 1978). In fact, one long-term study (Werner & Smith, 1982, 1992) showed that having a close, supportive relationship with a caregiver in early childhood was a "resiliency factor" for low income children of color. Those children who had experienced such a relationship were more likely to be well adjusted and self-sufficient in adolescence and adulthood than those without such a relationship. Other studies similarly report that the quality of children's early relationships with their providers in child care emerges as an important predictor of older school children's social relations with teachers and peers (Howes, Hamilton & Phillipsen, 1998; Howes & Tonyan, 2000), their behavior problems (Howes & Ritchie, 1999), and school satisfaction and achievement (Baker, 1999; Peisner-Feinberg et al., 1999). Children who are more emotionally secure with their provider in child care are better able to use the materials and resources available in the child care setting and to form competent and trusting relationships with peers when they are older (Howes & Hamilton, 1993; Howes & Smith, 1995).

Based on the theoretical links between emotional availability and attachment theory, and the evidence on the importance of attachment relationships in child care, extending the construct of emotional availability to child care providers seems appropriate. In fact, emotional availability may be elemental in understanding the impact of early learning experiences on children's concurrent and future developmental outcomes.

Recent Findings Using the EAS in Child Care Settings

Similar to extending attachment theory to child care research, EAS may also capture the quality of the provider-child relationship. Indeed, the authors of the EAS suggest researchers empirically test the use of EAS with non-parental caregivers (Easterbrooks & Biringen, 2000). As such, the second objective of this paper is to review four recent studies that have piloted the use of the EAS in various child care arrangements with demographically diverse samples of children and caregivers. One of the four is a published, albeit exploratory, study; the other three studies are unpublished. The studies reviewed extend the use of the EAS to a variety of child care settings. The child care arrangements described in this review include center-based care as well as home-based settings. Findings are organized and reviewed based on two different frameworks. First, an investment-model paradigm (Farrell & Rusbult, 1981; Whitebook, Howes, Phillips, & Pemberton, 1989) is applied to findings from three child care studies in which emotional availability was associated with professional investment variables like number of early childhood education (ECE) college courses, number of training workshops attended, and previous experience in a formal college early childhood program. The investment model proposes that individuals who actively invest in their vocation (e.g., education and on-going training) are more likely to become committed to their jobs and motivated to enhance the quality of their work (Farrell & Rusbult, 1981). Child care literature demonstrates that providers' education and on-going traning are important predictors of effective teaching in early childhood classrooms (Howes, Whitebook, & Phillips, 1992).

Second, a family-support paradigm (McLoyd, 1990) is applied to findings from another child care study in which emotional availability was predicted using variables such as perceived financial need, social support, and emotional well-being. According to the family-support model, the challenge of successfully raising children in poverty requires as many supportive resources as one can muster. Researchers using this model posit that emotional and social support may reduce parental stress – thereby impacting parental behavior and parent-child interactions. Organizing theses studies based on their frameworks highlights the broad applicability of the EAS in child care research.

Investment-Model Paradigm

The first study by Shivers (2004) was exploratory and focused on the interactional dimensions of informal child care arrangements (e.g., family, friend, neighbor care). The study involved informal child care providers living in low-income urban communities in Los Angeles (80% African American; 20% Latina). Emotional availability was measured using the EAS during a naturalistic observation lasting one to two hours in providers' homes. Forty-eight provider-child dyads were included in this study. In general, provider sensitivity as measured by the EAS appears associated with providers' ethnic background, professional educational background, provider-child engagement, and environmental quality. In other words, this study suggests that providers with higher sensitivity scores were likely Latina, had more education, engaged frequently with children, and provided a higher quality environment for the children in their care. This study highlights potential issues, such as cultural community and professional background, in the quality of child care provided by family, friends and neighbors.

The second study by Zajac, Farber, Shivers, and Barnard (2006) used the EAS in an evaluation of the effectiveness of a new child care training module (Mind in the Making, Families and Work Institute), which specifically emphasizes the importance of children's social and emotional development. Emotional availability was measured using the EAS during a 3-hour naturalistic observation in child care centers. This pre/post curriculum intervention evaluation design involved 17 child care providers in centers located in Pittsburgh, Pennsylvania. The providers in this study were mostly Caucasian (93%) and well educated (70% BA or higher). The authors of this study report that for providers who participated in the training modules there was an association between provider sensitivity (as measured by the EAS) and overall environmental quality scores (as measured by the Early Childhood Environmental Rating Scale – Revised; Harms, Clifford, & Cryer, 1998). Results suggest that investing in specialized provider training that focuses on children's social and emotional needs may enhance a program's quality of care.

The third study by Gmiter and Shivers (2008) was conducted in therapeutic preschools with children on the Autism spectrum and explored the relationship between emotional availability and child care providers' professional development background (e.g., formal education, amount and content of in-service specialized training). Emotional availability observations lasted 4 hours and took place in child care classrooms. This study involved nine child care providers and 31 children on the Autism spectrum. The children were classified as Caucasian (77.4%), African American (19.4%), and "other" (3.2%). All the child care providers in this study were Caucasian. The authors of this exploratory study report that those providers who reported receiving more in-service training on staff-support issues tended to score higher on Provider Structuring ratings and Provider Non-Hostility ratings (as measured by the EAS). Similarly, more provider-reported training on how to conduct child observations was associated with higher scores on Provider Structuring, and more optimal scores on Provider Non-Hostility ratings. Gmiter and Shivers suggest that more specialized training may be beneficial in helping teachers learn to implement behavioral interventions maximizing socialization experiences of children with Autism (Koegel, Russo, & Rincover, 1977; Laski, Charlop, & Schreibman, 1988).

Family Support Model Paradigm

The fourth study by Shivers and Kim (under review) explored attachment relationships between 46 low-income African American family, friend and neighbor child care providers and the children in their care. Emotional availability was measured using the EAS and attachment relationships were measured using the Attachment Q-Sort (Waters, 1990). The dyadic relationships were observed during 3-to 4-hour naturalistic observations, which took place in providers' homes. This study was informed by the adaptive cultural integrative (García Coll et al., 1996) and the family stress (McLoyd, 1990) models. As such, the study included some constructs previously measured only in a parental context (e.g., perceived financial need and EA). The authors suggest that because child care providers are similar to parents in terms of demographics and on-going emotional investment, predictors for provider-child interactions are likely comparable to predictors of parent-child interactions. The authors suggest that issues such as provider emotional well-being, perceived economic need, social support, childrearing beliefs, and EA may be related.

In the end, providers who display sensitive, non-hostile, structured, non-intrusive behaviors seem to form more secure positive relationships with children. This may hold true across income and ethnicity.

Implications

Emotional availability may emerge as relevant in the relationship between children's emotional development and child care. Ultimately, emotional availability may be useful in examining the impact of early care and learning settings on children's development. Thus, there are potential professional development, provider support, and child care measurement implications.

Professional development. The first three studies imply that professional investment variables (e.g., level of education, teaching experience, training workshops) are associated with emotional availability. This suggestion is consistent with child care studies linking professional educational experiences to sensitive, stimulating caregiving (Burchinal, Howes, & Kontos, 2002; Dunn, 1993; Fischer & Eheart, 1991; Howes, 1997; Howes, James, & Ritchie, 2003; Howes et al., 1992; Kontos, Howes, Shinn, & Galinsky, 1995; NICHD ECCRN, 1996; Whitebook et al., 1989). Thus, supporting child care providers' professional development appears significant in facilitating children's emotional development (Howes et al., 2003).

Provider support. The findings from the fourth study, albeit still under review, suggest that children's emotional development may be related to provider characteristics and beliefs. This study suggests that issues such as providers' perceived economic well-being, child-rearing beliefs, and emotional availability may be related. Indeed, other studies with parents show that poverty and income stress affect parenting values, practices and parent-child relationships (Duncan, Brooks-Gunn, & Klebanov, 1994; McLoyd & Wilson, 1990). More research is needed to assess the relationship between child care providers' social, material, and emotional needs and young children's emotional development.

Measuring quality of care. In an era of accountability and increasing awareness of children's experiences in early learning settings, the conversation about what constitutes *quality of care* is becoming more nuanced. In particular, defining and measuring child care quality may be difficult as definitions of quality vary across communities and families (Kontos et al., 1995; Shivers, 2004). For example, many child care investigations use standardized global measures of quality that are not necessarily sensitive to cultural variation or the fine-grained nature of children's relationships with their providers.

In the end, further research regarding emotional availability and child care is indicated. The EAS may emerge as an appropriate tool to investigate caregiver-child relationships and, perhaps, serve as a guide in developing research-based intervention programs supporting children's social-emotional development.

References

Ainsworth, M. D., Blehar, M. C., Waters, E., & Wall, S. (1978). *Patterns of attachment: A psychological study of the strange situation.* Hillsdale, NJ: Erlbaum.

Baker, J. A. (1999). Teacher-student interaction in urban at-risk classrooms: Differential behavior, relationship quality, and student satisfaction with school. *Elementary School Journal, 100,* 57-70.

Biringen, Z., & Robinson, J. (1991). Emotional availability: A reconceptualization for research. *American Journal of Orthopsychiatry, 61,* 258-271.

Biringen, Z., Robinson, J., & Emde, R. (2000). The Emotional Availability Scales (3rd ed.; an abridged infancy/early childhood version) [Special issue]. *Attachment and Human Development, 2,* 256-270.

Bowlby, J. (1969/1982). *Attachment and loss: Vol. 1. Attachment.* New York: Basic Books.

Bretherton, I. (1985). Attachment theory retrospect and prospect. *Monographs of the Society for Research in Child Development, 50,* 3-35.

Bretherton, I. (2000). Emotional availability: An attachment perspective [Special issue]. *Attachment and Human Development, 2,* 233-241.

Burchinal, M., Howes, C., & Kontos, S. (2002). Structural predictors of childcare quality in childcare homes. *Early Childhood Research Quarterly, 17,* 87-105.

Duncan, G. J., Brooks-Gunn, F., & Klebanov, P. (1994). Economic deprivation and early childhood development. *Child Development, 65,* 296-318.

Dunn, L. (1993). Proximal and distal features of childcare quality and children's development. *Early Childhood Research Quarterly, 8,* 167-192.

Easterbrooks, M. A., Biesecker, G., & Lyons-Ruth, K. (2000). Infancy predictors of emotional availability in middle childhood: The roles of attachment security and maternal depressive symptomatology. *Attachment and Human Development, 2,* 170-187.

Easterbrooks, M. A., & Biringen, Z. (2000). Introduction to the special issue: Mapping the terrain of emotional availability and attachment [Special issue]. *Attachment and Human Development, 2,* 123-129.

Easterbrooks, M. A., & Biringen, Z. (2005). The Emotional Availability Scales: Methodological refinements of the construct and clinical implications related to gender and at-risk interactions. *Infant Mental Health Journal, 26,* 291-294

Emde, R. N., & Easterbrooks, M. A. (1985). Assessing emotional availability in early development. In W. K. Frankenburg, R. N. Emde, & J. W. Sullivan (Eds.), *Early identification of children at risk: An international perspective* (pp. 79–101). New York: Plenum.

Farrell, D., & Rusbult, C. E. (1981). Exchange variables as predictors of job satisfaction, job commitment, and turnover: The impact of rewards, costs, alternatives, and investments. *Organizational Behavior and Human Performance, 27/28*, 78-95.

Fischer, J. L., & Eheart, B. K. (1991). Family day care: A theoretical basis for improving quality. *Early Childhood Research Quarterly, 6*, 549-563.

García Coll, C., Lamberty, G., Jenkins, R., McAdoo, H. P., Crnic, K., Wasik, B. H., & Garcia, H. V. (1996). An integrative model for the study of developmental competencies in minority children. *Child Development, 67*, 1891-1941.

Garmezy, N. (1993). Vulnerability and resilience. In D. C. Funder, R. D. Ross, C. E. Tomlinson-Keasey, & K. Widaman (Eds.), *Studying lives through time: Personality and development* (pp. 377-398). Washington, DC: American Psychological Association.

Gmiter, A., & Shivers, E. (2008). *Preschoolers in the autism spectrum: Exploring relationships, peer play, and teachers' professional experiences.* Manuscript submitted for publication.

Harms, T., Clifford, R., & Cryer, D. (1998). *Early Childhood Environmental Rating Scale, Revised Edition.* Vermont: Teachers College Press.

Howes, C. (1997). Children's experiences in center-based childcare as a function of teacher background and adult-child ratio. *Merrill-Palmer Quarterly, 43*, 404-425.

Howes, C. (1999). Attachment relationships in the context of multiple caregivers. In J. Cassidy & P. R. Shaver (Eds.), *Handbook of attachment: Theory, research and clinical applications* (pp. 671 -687). New York: Guilford Press.

Howes, C., & Hamilton, C. E. (1993). The changing experience of childcare: Changes in teachers and in teacher-child relationships and children's social competence with peers. *Early Childhood Research Quarterly, 8*, 15-32.

Howes, C., Hamilton, C. E., & Phillipsen, L. (1998). Stability and continuity of child-caregiver and child-peer relationships. *Child Development, 69*, 418-426.

Howes, C., James, J., & Ritchie, S. (2003). Pathways to effective teaching. *Early Childhood Research Quarterly, 18*, 104-120.

Howes, C., & Ritchie, S. (1999). Attachment organizations in children with difficult life circumstances. *Development and Psychopathology, 11*, 254-268.

Howes, C., & Ritchie, S. (2002). *A matter of trust: Connecting teachers and learners in the early childhood classroom.* New York: Teachers College Press.

Howes, C., & Shivers, E. M. (2006). New child-caregiver attachment relationships: Entering child care when the caregiver is and is not an ethnic match. *Social*

Development, 15, 574-590.

Howes, C., & Smith, E. (1995). Child care quality, teacher behavior, children's play activities, emotional security and cognitive activity in child care. *Early Childhood Research Quarterly, 10,* 381-404.

Howes, C., & Tonyan, H. (2000). Links between adult and peer relationship across four developmental periods. In K. A. Kerns & A. M. Neal-Barnett (Eds.), *Examining associations between parent-child and peer relationships* (pp. 143-157). New York: Greenwood/Praeger.

Howes, C., Whitebook, M., & Phillips, D. A. (1992). Teacher characteristics and effective teaching in childcare: Findings from the National Childcare Staffing Study. *Child and Youth Forum, 21,* 399-414.

Koegel, R. L., Russo, D. C., & Rincover, A. (1977). Assessing and training teachers in the generalized use of behavior modification with autistic children. *Journal of Applied Behavior Analysis, 10,* 197-206.

Kontos, S., Howes, C., Shinn, M., & Galinsky, E. (1995). *Quality in family childcare and relative care.* New York: Teachers College Press.

Lamb, M. E. (1998). Nonparental child care: Context, quality, and correlates. In W. Damon (Series Ed.) & I. E. Sigel & K. A. Renninger (Vol. Eds.), *Handbook of child psychology: Vol. 4. Child psychology in practice* (pp. 73-133). New York: John Wiley & Sons.

Laski, K. E., Charlop, M. H., & Schreibman, L. (1988). Training parents to use the natural language paradigm to increase their autistic children's speech. *Journal of Applied Behavior Analysis, 21,* 391-400.

Mahler, M. S., Pine, F., & Bergman, A. (1975). *The psychological birth of the human infant: Symbiosis and individuation.* New York: Basic Books.

McLoyd, V. C. (1990). The impact of economic hardship on Black families and children: Psychological distress parenting and socioemotional development. *Child Development, 61,* 311-346.

McLoyd, V. C., & Wilson, L. (1990). Maternal behavior, social support, and economic conditions as predictors of psychological distress in children. In V. C. McLoyd & C. Flanagan (Eds.), *New directions for child development. Economic stress: Effects on family life and child development* (pp. 49-69). San Francisco: Jossey-Bass.

Mitchell-Copeland, J., Denham, S., & DeMulder, E. (1997). Q-Sort assessment of child-teacher attachment relationships and social competence in the preschool. *Early Education and Development, 8,* 27-39.

Mubler, E. K., Denham, S., Schmidt, M., & Mitchell, J. (2000). Q-Sort assessment of attachment security during the preschool years: Links from home to school. *Developmental Psychology, 36,* 274-282.

NICHD Early Childcare Research Network. (1996). Characteristics of infant childcare: Factors contributing to positive caregiving. *Early Childhood Research Quarterly, 11,* 269-306.

NICHD Early Childcare Research Network. (1998). Relations between family predictors and child outcomes: Are they weaker for children in childcare? *Developmental Psychology, 34,* 1119-1128.

Pedersen, E., Faucher, T. A., & Eaton, W. W. (1978). A new perspective on the effects of first grade teachers on children's subsequent adult status. *Harvard Educational Review, 48,* 1-31.

Peisner-Feinberg, E., Burchinal, M., Clifford, R., Culkin, M., Howes, C., & Kagan, S. L. (1999). *The children from the Cost Quality and Outcome Study go to school.* Public Report. Denver CO: Center for Research on Economic and Social Policy.

Pianta, R. C., Hamre, B., & Stuhlman, M. (Eds.). (2002). *Relationships between teachers and children* (Vol. 7). New York: Wiley.

Pianta, R. C., Steinberg, M. S., & Rollins, K. B. (1995). The first two years of school: Teacher-child relationships and deflections in children's classroom adjustment. *Development and Psychopathology, 7,* 295-312.

Shivers, E. M. (2004). A closer look at kith and kin care: Exploring variability of quality within family, friend and neighbor care. *Applied Developmental Psychology, 27,* 411-426.

Shivers, E. M., & Kim, K. H. (2008). *Provider-child attachment relationships in family, friend and neighbor care: Understanding the contribution of African American caregiver characteristics, beliefs and behavior.* Manuscript submitted for publication.

Shonkoff, J. P., & Phillips, D. A. (Eds.) (2000). *From neurons to neighborhoods.* Washington, DC: National Academy Press.

Waters, E. (1990). *The Attachment Q-Set.* Unpublished manuscript, State University of New York at Stony Brook.

Werner, E. E., & Smith, R. S. (1982). *Vulnerable but invincible: A longitudinal study of resilient children and youth.* New York: McGraw-Hill.

Werner, E. E., & Smith, R. S. (1992). *Overcoming the odds: High risk children from birth to adulthood.* Ithaca, NY: Cornell University Press.

Wishard, A., Shivers, E. M., Howes, C., & Ritchie, S. (2003). Childcare program and teacher practices: Associations with quality and children's experiences. *Early Childhood Research Quarterly, 18,* 65-103.

Zajac, J., Farber, A., Shivers, E. M., & Barnard, W. (2006). *Evaluation Report: Mind in the Making Learning Modules for early childhood teachers in Pennsylvania.* Prepared for Families and Work Institute with support of the Heinz Endowments.

Ziv, Y., Aviezer, O., Gini, M., Sagi, A., & Koren-Karie, N. (2000). Emotional availability in the mother-infant dyad as related to the quality of infant-mother attachment relationship. *Attachment and Human Development, 2,* 149-169.

The Emotional Availability (EA) Intervention with Child Care Professionals

Zeynep Biringen, Albertha Moorlag, Beatrice Meyer, Judi Wood, Jennifer Aberle, Shannon Altenhofen, & Sera Bennett
Colorado State University

After almost a decade of basic science research on the Emotional Availability Scales, an intervention program based on the assessment instrument was developed. The intervention involves the training of parents and professional development for child care providers regarding attachment concepts and emotional availability, including both informational and experiential components. This paper describes the professional development program for child care professionals of infants and toddlers who are in child care centers at least 20 hours a week. It was proposed that attachment and emotional availability training for child care professionals would enhance their professional development related to children and improve the relational and emotional atmosphere of center-based care.

The biological basis for attachment is the instinct to survive and seek protection during the vulnerable stages of infancy and early childhood. Thus, according to Bowlby (1980), attachment behaviors are observed across all cultures and throughout an individual's development. Approximately 70% of infants are secure in their attachments with their parents, while 30% tend to be insecure. These percentages apply to all economic backgrounds, cultural groups, mothers, and fathers in the United States (Bakermans-Kranenburg, van Ijzendoorn, & Juffer, 2003; Biringen, 2004).

Researchers have studied attachment relationships for over 40 years, with the focus primarily on mothers (Biringen, 2004). Infant attachment security to the mother has been found to be predictive of later positive affect with preschool classmates and competence in school-age peer interactions (e.g., ego-resiliency, popularity with classmates, less social anxiety) (Bohlin, Hagekull, & Rydell, 2000; Waters, Wippman, & Sroufe, 1979). Securely attached infants and their mothers also show more positive interactions dur-

All correspondence should be addressed to Zeynep Biringen, Department of Human Development & Family Studies, Colorado State University, Fort Collins, CO 80523. Electronic mail may be sent to biringen@CAHS.Colostate.edu.

ing joint book reading than insecurely attached infants (Bus & van Izjen-doorn, 1992).

Importance of Child Care Professionals as Attachment Figures and Relationship Partners

Almost two decades ago, Goosens and van Ijzendoorn (1990) indicated the importance of caregivers other than the mother as attachment figures. Calculations from the 1999 National Survey of America's Families (NSAF) show that approximately half (48%) of mothers were in the workforce full-time (Urban Institute and Child Trends, 1999). Currently, 39% of children in the United States, and 36% of children under the age of 3, are spending 35 or more hours in center-based child care per week. Given the large numbers of infants in child care and particularly those who are at least half-time in child care, the quality of relationships with not only the mother but also with the child care provider becomes a particularly important area of investigation.

Child care providers spend considerable amounts of time with the children in their care, and these relationships may offset varying social risk factors, such as teen parenting, caregiver chemical dependency, domestic violence, and/or parenting practices that are associated with negative child outcomes. Under such circumstances, child care providers may serve as a buffer to the primary attachment relationships with parents and thereby enhance a child's overall adjustment. In addition, child care providers may be able to partner with parents in an emotionally connected way and even provide role modeling for optimal adult-child interactions (Marty, Readdick, & Walters, 2005; Spieker, Nelson, Petras, Jolley, & Barnard, 2003; Zimmerman & Fassler, 2003). In fact, among children not securely attached to their parents, Howes and her colleagues report compensatory attachments to teachers (Howes, Rodning, Galluzzo, & Myers, 1988).

Further, research supports the assertion that relationships with child care providers/teachers can predict children's social-emotional development. For example, Howes, Hamilton, and Matheson (1994) found that for children in child care, attachment with child care providers/teachers was a better predictor of peer relationships than attachment to mothers.

Given the importance of child care providers/teachers to the large number of infants and young children in child care, understanding the quality of these relationships is becoming increasingly important. Howes and Smith (1995) report that although 68% of infants are securely attached to their mothers (and fathers), only 50% of children are securely attached to their child care providers/teachers. This finding suggests that at least 50% of children in half-time child care may not be spending a large portion of their early development in an emotionally secure context.

Reviews of child care quality show that standards vary widely, and the majority of child care settings may fail to provide children with appropriate stimulation and emotional support (Howes & Smith, 1995). Increased education of care providers has been linked with higher quality interactions between child care providers and children (Arnett, 1989). Further, children in classrooms where providers are more educated have been found to be more advanced in their language skills (Burchinal, Cryer, Clifford, & Howes, 2002). However, many care providers report a number of impediments to continuing education, with inconvenient scheduling being reported by caregivers as being a significant barrier, in addition to distance, cost, quality, and inadequate notice of training (Gable & Halliburton, 2003).

Just as caregiver sensitivity is a crucial component of parent-child attachment relationships (Ainsworth, Blehar, Waters, & Wall, 1978), sensitivity is also a key aspect of provider/teacher-child interactions. Research reveals that when child care providers are sensitive and responsive the children exhibit behaviors indicative of security and tend to interact with emotional availability (Zimmerman & Fassler, 2003). Training child care providers to become more sensitive in their interactions at child care sites has been found to be effective in enhancing sensitivity and in improving children's attachments (Howes, Galinsky, & Kontos, 1998).

The Emotional Availability (EA) Framework

The construct of "emotional availability" is more comprehensive than the construct of sensitivity. To assess the construct of emotional availability, the EA Scales (Biringen, Robinson, & Emde, 1998) were developed. As conceptualized by Biringen, emotional availability and EA[1] refer to a suite of instruments and products. EA is used consistently throughout this manuscript to refer to Biringen's measurements and programs based on the emotional availability construct. Thus, EA includes four caregiver dimensions (i.e., caregiver sensitivity, structuring, nonintrusiveness, nonhostility) and two child dimensions (i.e., child responsiveness to the caregiver, child attempts to involve the caregiver).

EA offers the possibility of a multi-faceted look at caregiver-child interactions that includes, as well as goes beyond, sensitivity to reflect more differentiated caregiver constructs as well as the child's contribution to the relationship. Thus, in addition to caregiver sensitivity, the ability to structure and set limits, be nonintrusive, and manage anger and hostility in relationships are deemed important.

---

[1] Emotional Availability (EA) as well as emotional availability have been trademarked and refer to the use of the Emotional Availability Scales or its derivative suite of instruments and products in research or practice. More information on EA, including the full checklist, may be found at: www.emotionalavailability.com or by writing Biringen at zbiringen@yahoo.com.

In addition to the multi-dimensional framework, another asset of EA is that two dimensions specifically address child qualities (i.e., child responsiveness to caregiver, child's attempts to involve caregiver), thus capturing not only the adult's side of the relationship, but also the child's. Further, these child qualities are not based on inborn temperament or individual child characteristics, but are the product of the relationship between the caregiver and child, reflecting the dynamic nature of that particular relationship.

Emotional availability is related to but different from the attachment concept. Emotional availability is found in distress and stress situations, like attachment, but is also relevant in a whole variety of interactions, including play. For example, emotional availability encompasses the caregiver's ability to express genuine and spontaneous emotions with the child, and for the child to express genuine and spontaneous emotions with the caregiver. According to Biringen (2000), emotional availability also encompasses the willingness of a provider to comprehend the emotional experience being expressed by the child. On one level, it can be conceptualized as the mutual expression of emotional responses between the caregiver and the child. On another level, emotional availability may represent a relationship network. Although emotional availability is thought of as mutual emotional expressiveness, this does not imply that related abilities (e.g., accurate perception and interpretation of emotional content) between the parties (i.e., caregiver, child) are equivalent. Clearly, and more to the point, the adult in the relationship has a vast array of emotional experiences involving a host of relationships and meanings which the child does not.

With these developmental issues in mind, the six qualities of EA are dimensions and not thought of as classifications. Thus, all individuals are thought to have some level of emotional availability and, further, these qualities can be improved.

The EA Intervention For Parents and Professional Caregivers

After nearly a decade of research on emotional availability (Aviezer, Sagi, Joels, & Ziv, 1999; Biringen et al., 2005; Bornstein, Gini, Leach, et al., 2006; Bornstein, Gini, Suwalsky, et al., 2006; Easterbrooks & Biringen, 2000; Easterbrooks & Biringen, 2005), the EA related concepts were used to develop an intervention program. The EA intervention has both parent and non-parental/professional caregiver components. At present, the parent component is delivered in a group format, focusing on information and video discussions of the relationship of each parent with each child in the family. The non-parental caregiver component also is delivered in a group format, but adds one-on-one interactive EA coaching, to provide additional practice for the professionals in their place of work. In this article on child care, we describe solely the professional development component.

Description of the EA Intervention

Group Format Training

Providers were given group-format psychoeducational training on types of attachment as well as the link between dyadic interactions and each type of attachment. This training was done through sharing of written material as well as 2 hours of classroom instruction. When providers were unable to attend the university-based instruction, the information was delivered to them in small group settings at their site.

Prior to the group psychoeducational training, the initial 2 hours of each filmed observation was evaluated using the EA Scales and the Attachment Q-Set (AQS; Waters & Deane, 1985). As a result, a determination of each child's attachment pattern was made during the subsequent psychoeducational training, each child-provider pairing, and the child attachment types were discussed (secure, insecure/avoidant/emotionally shut down, and insecure/resistant/emotionally demanding, as described below). The providers were enlisted as "interventionists" for children with problematic attachments and as agents to maintain security for those children viewed as well adjusted. Key aspects of the information provided were the three main types of attachment, as might be observed in the child care context. These three types are as follows:

1. *Secure.* Child looks happy at the center and interacts well with the provider. In this case, the provider's responsibility at the center is to maintain attachment security, by continuing to be high in emotional availability (e.g., engaging in regular play times with the child, including the child in interactions with other children, keeping the child engaged and involved in the classroom). Child care is emphasized as a challenging context for all infants and providers are encouraged to continue engaging in positive interaction with these children.

2. *Insecure/Avoidant/Emotionally shut down.* Child looks shut down, may look as if s/he does not need others, and may appear "weakly attached" to others. S/he may be mistaken for an "easy" child and therefore may not receive attention in the midst of a multiple children context. These children need attention, but may not feel comfortable or be accustomed to seeking attention. In this case, the provider works to create trusting, interactional cycles with this child, deliberately seeking out, elaborating, and prolonging such interactions and exchanges.

3. *Insecure/Resistant/Emotionally demanding.* Child cries/demands attention through negative behaviors and may seem "strongly attached" to the provider; some providers comment positively on these behaviors, seeing the behaviors as a positive child attribute. Through guided discussion, the provider may begin realizing that child clinginess is related to a lack of security and these children need to gain confidence and develop self-efficacy. In this instance, the provider's job is to foster a sense of security over time. The system described was used flexibly to discuss

relationship quality and assist providers in thinking about children in child care in a number of ways, such as healthy interdependence as opposed to extreme self-reliance. Although interdependent and overly self-reliant children may both appear easy in temperament they may benefit from different caregiver behaviors. Thus, the system was used to assist providers in thinking about children, in relation to children's behaviors. For example, children who demand a great deal of attention through clingy and demanding behaviors may be rewarding the behaviors of their preferred attachment figures. Providers often need extra support in differentiating healthy behavior from emotionally unhealthy behaviors associated with insecure attachment.

EA Coaching

In addition to the group psychoeducational training, each child care provider was provided with individual EA coaching. Prior to the coaching, the EA Checklist (see next section, Active Ingredients of the EA Intervention) was shared with each target provider. The EA Checklist describes verbal and nonverbal indicators of each of the EA dimensions, as might be seen in a child care site. The providers were given a chance to study and familiarize themselves with the EA Checklist as part of homework, prior to the start of coaching.

Each of the four EA coaches was assigned specific target providers and they conducted each of the sessions with them. A single EA coach conducted the on-site, interactive training with a specific provider. Forming a close, connected, emotionally available relationship with the target provider could only happen in the context of a dedicated relationship. Two EA coaches had extensive prior experience in coaching child care providers, were members of the community's Early Childhood Council, and were early care and education leaders in the community and state. Both were trained in EA through the Biringen EA training tapes, although not to the level of reliability needed for research scoring. The third EA coach was a master's student in a graduate human development and family studies program and the fourth a doctoral student in a marriage and family therapy program. Although the backgrounds were diverse for this initial intervention and a more formal and streamlined EA training for the coaches has been developed for our upcoming work, each coach had two of the four components of what we consider to be acceptable qualifications for a coach: (a) a graduate degree, (b) extensive experience in the community as well as in child care, (c) therapy training and experience, and (d) knowledge and training in EA principles.

The EA coaching begins by visits to the sites and getting to know the target children and the target provider. The coaching has four components:

1. Quiet watching and participant observation at the sites: There is no rush to say something or become involved. The coaches are attentive (e.g., watching the tape with the child care provider in an interested and engaged way).

2. Supporting the target provider in a strengths-based approach: The coach

makes a mental note of the strengths in a particular target provider's style and begins there. Subsequently, the coach leaves a report of the provider's strengths using the EA Checklist and this process continues after each session with the provider. Often, the EA structuring dimension is a place to find strengths, even where a target provider is new to the profession and is described by the EA coach as at a beginning point for intervention. Often, with the first EA Checklist/written narrative, providers sense they know a great deal and that the coach will be supportive of them in finding ways to deal with children's challenging behaviors or in supporting their enjoyment of the children served.

3. Videoplayback is brought into the program at a point when the target provider has engaged in a few sessions over the course of two weeks. The video from the pre-test is shown and often the target providers are amazed to see that they have moved beyond that level in their repertoire of skills with the children. The videoplayback starts with and consists of quiet watching, with the target provider describing what they see and what they are thinking about further emotional connection with the children.

4. The coach introduces the idea of "magic moments" (to be described further, below) and discusses how magic moments can be used to move insecurely attached children toward security. There is no fixed sequence to the introduction.

Active Ingredients of the EA Intervention

EA Checklist

As mentioned above, after each visit, the coach completes notes on the EA Checklist as a means to communicate with the provider about EA (Biringen, 2005a). The EA Checklist presents specific behaviors associated with healthy emotional availability toward children. See Figure 1 for a sample excerpt from the EA Checklist.

For each of the EA dimensions, what follows are descriptions of specific indicators of higher levels of each of the qualities tapped by the checklist. The EA coach simply checks off the qualities he or she perceives at a particular visit to the child care center and provides written notes about the interactions observed on that day. The checklist serves as a way for the coach to communicate in detail and in a lasting way with the provider.

Sensitivity – When near child, provider touches child's head or shoulder, gives warm hugs, smiles, seems nicely relaxed, interacts in a genuine and enthusiastic way, does not ignore other children when focused on the target child, treats child as special.

Structuring – Sets up appropriate activities, talks to child and structures changes through verbalization, helps child learn emotion words by using them when talking with child.

Figure 1
Example of Partly Completed EA Checklist

Nonhostility: nonverbal level

___ Tries not to feel bored

_X_ Does not seem overwhelmed and stressed; uses smiling and breathing exercises to take care of herself/himself

_X_ Hugs and works to soothe other babies if distressed, creating greater peace in the room

_X_ Does not ignore babies/toddlers in distress and responds without a delay, suggesting "You are number 1."

This provider is doing a much better job of "self care" (because she seems to know that without taking care of herself, she will not be able to regulate her affect) and tries to take her breaks on time to "recharge" for the kids. Provider responded to a crying child in the background right away and held her on her lap till she was calm—I could see that this affection really helped the other kids to calm down, too. Good for you!

Nonintrusiveness – Picks up child in gentle manner, minimizes intrusions on child by verbalizing interventions, plays with child where child is playing, uses gentle words to direct negative behaviors, comments on what child is doing, and says please and thank you.

Nonhostility – Tries not to seem stressed (e.g., she breathes deeply to relieve tension), responds readily and soothes children in distress, hugs child when appropriate, and does not complain even when it is a rough day.

The coach watches behaviors between the provider and the child and then mentors the provider in expressing and maintaining all levels of emotional availability. If children have a secure attachment bond, maintenance of that bond is important across all caretaker environments (e.g., child care, preschool). Even if insecure at home, children may experience a secure connection with another caregiver. Because secure attachment is related to children's later psychosocial development, child care presents an opportunity for facilitating emotional growth by enlisting the help of child care providers, child care directors, and parents.

Magic Moments

The provider is trained to respond to the child's unique needs by the use of "magic moments," a term we coined to describe a moment in which the adult sees an opportunity to alter an existing pattern of insecure attachment. The point of the activities is to turn the child's trust around and establish a more secure attachment. A magic moment is a special moment just between the provider and the child (e.g., the provider holds eye contact, a genuine smile toward the child). Magic moments are the link that creates an emotional pathway between the provider and the child. These moments may facilitate an attachment relationship between the provider and child even if none seemed to exist or redirect a relationship toward a secure connection when the connection seemed to be based on dependency. The special relationship created by these magic moments helps to establish emotional availability in each relationship. The provider is empowered during the training to recognize opportunities to make a difference in a toddler's life by being emotionally available. The specific type of magic moment the provider works to create is based on the specific type of child attachment (e.g., a child who seems to be insecure/avoidant would receive longer and more engaged periods of interaction or play with the child care provider).

Pre-test/Post-test Assessments

Pre-tests were conducted by the assessment team with each identified pair of target provider and target child. Pre-tests involved 2 hours of observation (1/2 hour of filming and an additional 1-½ hours of direct observation). Soon after the intervention, the post-test was scheduled and conducted, with post-test assessments identical to those of the pre-test.

The child care provider-child relationships were examined through the lens of two assessments, the EA Scales (Biringen et al., 1998) and the AQS (Waters & Deane, 1985). The EA Scales were scored on the 1/2 hour of film and the AQS was scored on the ½ hour of film plus 1-½ hours of direct observation (the ½ hour of film is used during EA Coaching and the AQS is used for the understanding of attachment styles). Graduate students conducted the AQS assessments and the EA Scales' scoring. Scorers of the EA Scales were blind to AQS assessments. EA training was conducted by the use of the Biringen training tapes (Biringen, 2005b), followed by individual training, with initial reliability at $r = .85$. AQS training was conducted and reliability was checked after every visit, maintained at approximately $r = .80$.

The Emotional Availability (EA) Scales. The EA framework (Biringen, 2000), which emphasizes both caregiver and child perspectives, was used to understand the child care provider-child dyadic relationship. EA is somewhat global and focuses on the target child as well as the target caregiver. The outcome measures are of the child (i.e., child responsiveness, child involvement) and of the caregiver in relationship with a particular child (i.e., EA sensitivity, EA structuring, EA non-intrusiveness, EA nonhostility). Numerous studies have established the construct validity of the instrument, including in international contexts (e.g., Aviezer et al., 1999; Bornstein, Gini, Leach et al., 2006; Bornstein, Gini, Suwalsky et al., 2006; Easterbrooks & Biringen, 2000; Easterbrooks & Biringen, 2005).

The Attachment Q-Set. The Attachment Q-Set (AQS; Waters & Deane, 1985) is a system for measuring the quality of the attachment relationship between a specific caregiver and specific child in naturalistic settings. Given the extensive reliability and validity information on the AQS (e.g., Posada, Waters, Crowell, & Lay, 1995; Vaughn & Waters, 1990), the question was whether the instrument could be extended to the child care context of multiple caregivers and multiple children. In contrast to the EA Scales, which tend to measure the global or wholistic quality of the relationships between a caregiver and child, the AQS focuses on discrete, specific child characteristics. The AQS outcome measures (i.e., Security, Dependency) refer to the child's side of the relationship. The Security and Dependency composites were developed by following the algorithm described by Waters and Deane (1985).

Brief Summary of the Initial Investigation and Empirical Findings

Child care centers for infants and toddlers were recruited to participate in this project. No family child care homes were included. Directors at 10 sites consented to participate and letters of approval were obtained from each of these directors. Subsequently, individual child care providers were contacted and asked to participate. Although over 80% (17 caregivers paired with 32 infants/toddlers) of the providers initially agreed to participate, sometimes only one or two providers at a site ultimately participated. A drawback to participation was that interactions were videotaped. In addition to obtaining informed consent from each individual provider, informed consent was obtained from the parents of each child. Again, for both provider and family, consent was voluntary and the intervention proceeded only after obtaining consent for both.

All providers and families at each of the 10 infant/toddler sites (with a child attending child care at least 20 hours a week) were invited to participate. Recruitment letters and consent forms were sent home with all families. All providers were also given consent forms to read carefully and bring back to the center director. Through this process, 17 providers and 32 children were included in the study. Each provider was paired with 1 to 4 children. All children were between the ages of 11-33 months. Families were diverse in educational and socioeconomic backgrounds, with mother's education ranging from high school to a professional degree. The providers were also diverse in terms of educational backgrounds, ranging from high school to a college degree.

A randomized block design (Federer, 1991) was used to examine changes from pre- to post-test for the intervention group. Results indicated that both the child care providers and the children showed significant improvements in most dimensions of emotional availability from pre- to post-intervention (all dimensions except nonhostility showed improvements and base levels of this dimension were low at the start of the intervention). More detailed empirical examination of changes are summarized in Biringen et al. (2006) and Biringen et al. (2007) as part of the accumulating evidence base for this program.

New Directions

Potential applications of the EA intervention include use in a myriad of early care and education contexts (e.g., home settings, center-based care). Child care professionals may be trained to become more emotionally available, with the goal of enhancing attachment security in children and emotional availability in both the children and the caregiver.

This intervention for non-parental caregivers would be valuable in less normative contexts, such as for foster parents; substance-abusing, non-custodial mothers; and caregivers in residential treatment facilities. In each of these situations, the intervention may help the caregivers meet the needs of parents and/or children who present interactional challenges.

References

Ainsworth, M. D. S., Blehar, M., Waters, E., & Wall, S. (1978). *Patterns of attachment: A psychological study of the strange situation.* Hillsdale, NJ: Erlbaum.

Arnett, J. (1989). Caregivers in day-care centers: Does training matter? *Journal of Applied Developmental Psychology, 10*, 541-552.

Aviezer, O., Sagi, A., Joels, T., & Ziv, Y. (1999). Emotional availability and attachment representations in kibbutz infants and their mothers. *Developmental Psychology, 35*, 811-821.

Bakermans-Kranenburg, M. J., van Ijzendoorn, M. H., & Juffer, F. (2003). Less is more: Meta-analyses of sensitivity and attachment interventions in early childhood, *Pychological Bulletin, 129*, 195-215.

Biringen, Z. (2000). Emotional availability: Conceptualization and research findings. *American Journal of Orthopsychiatry, 70*(1), 104-114.

Biringen, Z. (2004). *Raising a secure child: Creating emotional connection between you and your child.* New York: Penguin.

Biringen, Z. (2005a). Emotional Availability (EA) Checklist. Unpublished, available from Biringen.

Biringen, Z. (2005b). Training and reliability issues with the Emotional Availability Scales. *Infant Mental Health Journal, 26* (4), 404-405.

Biringen, Z., Aberle, J., Altenhofen, S., Bennett, S., Meyer, B., & Moorlag, A. (2006, July). The Emotional Availability (EA) Intervention for child care providers of infants. In A. E. Easterbrooks & Z. Biringen (Co-Chairs), *Emotional availability: Cultural and community contexts.* Symposium conducted at the World Association for Infant Mental Health, Paris, France.

Biringen, Z., Damon, J., Grigg, W., Mone, J., Pipp-Siegel, S., Skillern, S., &

Stratton, J. (2005). Emotional availability: Differential predictions to infant attachment and kindergarten adjustment based on observation time and context. *Infant Mental Health Journal, 26,* 295-308.

Biringen, Z., Moorlag, A., Meyer, B., Wood, J., Aberle, J., Altenhofen, S., & Bennett, S. (2007, March). *The Emotional Availability(EA) Intervention.* In A. E. Easterbrooks & Z. Biringen (Co-Chairs), Child Care and Relationships. Symposium conducted at the Annual Meeting of the Society for Research in Child Development, Boston, MA.

Biringen, Z., Robinson, J., & Emde, R. N. (1998). *The Emotional Availability Scales (3rd ed.).* Unpublished manuscript, Department of Human Development & Family Studies, Colorado State University, Fort Collins, CO.

Bohlin, G., Hagekull, B., & Rydell, A. M. (2000). Attachment and social functioning: A longitudinal study from infancy to middle childhood. *Social Development, 9,* 24-39.

Bornstein, M. H., Gini, M., Leach, D. B., Haynes, O. M., Painter, K. M., & Suwalsky, J. T. D. (2006). Short-term reliability and continuity of emotional availability in mother-child dyads across contexts of observation. *Infancy, 10,* 1-16.

Bornstein, M. H., Gini, M., Suwalsky, J. T. D., Putnick, D. L., & Haynes, O. M. (2006). Emotional availability in mother-child dyads: Short-term stability and continuity from variable-centered and person-centered perspectives. *Merrill Palmer Quarterly*, 52, 547-571.

Bowlby, J. (1980). *Attachment.* New York: Basic Books.

Burchinal, M. R., Cryer, D., Clifford, R. M., & Howes, C. (2002). Caregiver training and classroom quality in child care centers. *Applied Developmental Science, 6,* 2-11.

Bus, A. G., & van Ijzendoorn, M. H. (1992). Patterns of attachment in frequently and infrequently reading dyads. *Journal of Genetic Psychology, 153,* 395-403.

Easterbrooks, A., & Biringen, Z. (2000). Mapping the terrain of emotional availability and attachment. *Attachment and Human Development, 2,* 129-135.

Easterbrooks, A. E., & Biringen, Z. (2005). The Emotional Availability Scales: Methodological refinements of the construct and clinical implications related to gender and at-risk interactions. *Infant Mental Health Journal, 26,* 291-294.

Federer, W. T. (1991). *Statistics and society.* New York: Marcel Dekker, Inc.

Gable, S., & Halliburton, A. (2003). Barriers to child care providers' professional development. *Child & Youth Care Forum, 32,* 175-193.

Goosens, F. A., & van Ijzendoorn, M. H. (1990). Quality of infants' attachments of professional caregivers—relation to infant-parent attachment and day-care characteristics. *Child Development, 61,* 832-837.

Howes, C., Galinsky, E., & Kontos, S. (1998). Child care caregiver sensitivity and attachment. *Social Development, 7(1),* 25-36.

Howes, C., Hamilton, C. E., & Matheson, C. E. (1994). Maternal, teacher, and child care history correlates of children's relationships with peers. *Child Development, 65,* 264-273.

Howes, C., Rodning, C., Galluzzo, D. C., & Myers, L. (1988). Attachment and child care relationships with mother and caregiver. *Early Childhood Research Quarterly, 3,* 403-416.

Howes, C., & Smith, E. W. (1995). Children and their child care caregivers: Profiles of relationships. *Social Development, 4,* 44-61.

Marty, A. H., Readdick, C. A., & Walters, C. M. (2005). Supporting secure parent-child attachments: The role of the non-parental caregiver. *Early Childhood Development and Care, 175(3),* 271-283.

Posada, G., Waters, E., Crowell, J., & Lay, K. L. (1995). Is it easier to use a secure mother as a secure base? Attachment Q-sort correlates of the adult attachment interview. *Monographs of the Society for Research in Child Development, 60,* 133-145.

Spieker, S. J., Nelson, D. C., Petras, A., Jolley, S. N., & Barnard, K. E. (2003). Joint influence of child care and infant attachment security for cognitive and language outcomes of low-income toddlers. *Infant Behavior and Development, 26,* 326-244.

Urban Institute and Child Trends. (1999). *National Survey of America's Families.* Washington, DC: Westat.

Vaughn, B., & Waters, E. (1990). Attachment behavior at home and in the laboratory: Q-sort observations and strange situation classifications of one-year-olds. *Child Development, 61,* 1965-1973.

Waters, E., & Deane, K. (1985). Defining and assessing individual differences in attachment relationships: Q-methodology and the organization of behavior in infancy and early childhood. *Monographs of the Society for Research in Child Development, 50,* 41-65.

Waters, E., Wippman, J., & Sroufe, L. (1979). Attachment, positive affect, and competence in the peer group: Two studies in construct validation. *Child Development, 50,* 821-829.

Zimmerman, L., & Fassler, I. (2003). The dynamics of emotional availability in child care: How infants involve and respond to their teen mothers and child care teachers. *Infants and Young Children, 16,* 258-269.

Author Note

We thank the study children, families, and child care professionals. Without them this study would not have happened. The project was funded by the Temple Hoyne Buell Foundation and the Bohemian Foundation.

Enhancing Parent-Provider Relationships and Communication in Infant and Toddler Classrooms

Mallary I. Swartz & M. Ann Easterbrooks
Tufts University

This study examined whether a relationships-based intervention for child care providers enhanced the quality of parent-provider relationships and communication as perceived by parents, and whether characteristics of providers and families were associated with change in these perceptions. A pre-test/post-test comparison design was used to assess key constructs at baseline and at approximately 6 months post-intervention. Parents of infants and toddlers ($N = 94$) from 14 child care centers (8 intervention and 6 comparison sites) completed the Parent Caregiver Partnership Scale, the Parent Caregiver Relationship Scale, and reported on satisfaction with provider-parent communication. The intervention was effective in enhancing parents' perceptions of their relationships with child care providers, especially for parents with less education and lower income. Parents who remained with the same caregiver over the 6-month time span also reported greater improvement in their relationships and satisfaction with communication with their children's child care providers than parents who did not remain with the same caregivers. Implications for continuity of care and training practices in early child care and education centers are discussed.

Young children develop in the context of their relationships with important others in their environments: parents, child care providers, and peers. Moreover, the quality of these relationships has implications for children's adaptation in other contexts. A large body of research, for example, has established the links between attachment relationships with parents and other aspects of children's development (Sroufe, Egeland, Carlson, & Collins, 2005; Thompson, 1999). The focus of the present study is on the relationships between the important adults in a young child's

All correspondence should be addressed to Mallary Swartz or M. Ann Easterbrooks, Eliot-Pearson Department of Child Development, Tufts University, Medford, MA 02155. Electronic mail may be sent to mallary.swartz@tufts.edu or ann.easterbrooks@tufts.edu.

social world, parents and child care providers, and on the effectiveness of an intervention designed to enhance these relationships.

Young children's social networks commonly extend beyond their families, to include non-familial caregivers (Burchinal et al., 2000). Over half of children under the age of 5 in the United States are cared for in child care centers or family child care homes, spending a considerable amount of time with other caregivers. Children of employed mothers spend an average of 34 hours per week in such settings (U.S. Department of Education, 2006). Children's relationships with caregivers can play an important role in their development. Similar to parent-child relationships, secure attachments to child care providers are linked with greater social competence and more positive peer interactions and more sophisticated play and cognitive development (Hamre & Pianta, 2001; Howes, Hamilton, & Matheson, 1994; Howes, Matheson, & Hamilton, 1994; Pianta & Stuhlman, 2004).

Although parent-child relationships generally remain stable, such is not the case for relationships between children and their child care providers. In center-based child care, for example, children change providers regularly, as they "age out" of a classroom. While this is common practice, some research has emphasized the importance of continuity of care (Hegde & Cassidy, 2004; Shonkoff & Phillips, 2000; Whitebook, Sakai, & Howes, 2004) finding that when children remain with the same providers over several years, they show more attachment-related behavior, more stable attachment to their caregivers (Barnas & Cummings, 1994; Howes & Hamilton, 1992), more socially competent peer interactions (Howes, Hamilton, & Matheson, 1994), and better school adjustment (e.g., fewer behavior problems, less school failure) into the elementary school years (Hofferth, Shauman, Henke & West, 1998; Howes, 1988; Howes & Hamilton, 1992). Essa, Favre, Thweatt, and Waugh (1999) asserted that continuity of care is especially important for infants and toddlers:

> One of the most important needs of infants and toddlers is for regular, predictable caregiving which allows [them] to develop a special relationship with a familiar adult. Taking away a consistent caregiver during the first 2 or 3 years of life compromises the sense of trust, the process of separation and the formation of a stable identity (p. 12).

Continuity of care also may play an important role in the development of relationships between child care providers and parents. Essa and her colleagues (1999) asserted "When the child remains with the same teacher for a 3-year period...trust and mutual respect [between parents and teachers] not only continue but grow" (p. 15). Further, parent-provider relationships play an important role in young children's development and experiences in child care. As Owen, Ware, and Barfoot (2000) stated, the "child's quality of experience in each environment may be enhanced when parent and child-care provider bridge the distance between the two social worlds of child care and home and work together as partners in the child's care" (p. 426).

Research on parent-provider relationships in child care largely stems from Bronfenbrenner's (2001) ecological systems theory, which views children's development as a product of the interactions that take place within the multiple environments in which they live. According to this view,

> the developmental potential of a setting is enhanced when the role demands in the different settings are compatible, there is goal consensus between settings, and there are supportive linkages between settings, including frequent two-way communication and parental participation in the child's entry into a new setting (Powell, 1997, p. 151).

Positive associations have been found between quality of parent-provider relationships and provider attitudes about parental competence, parents' experiences with child care, program quality, and children's development and experiences in child care.

Child care providers' attitudes about parents may be related to the overall quality of their relationships, and in turn, to parents' experiences with child care. For example, Kontos and Wells (1986) found that providers seemed to have more personal relationships with mothers who they felt were doing a good job as parents than with mothers who they felt were not. They also reported that low-esteemed mothers were less likely to see child care as a source of information about children and/or parenting. In a follow-up study, high-esteemed mothers reported more daily conversations with their children's child care providers and were more satisfied with care than low-esteemed mothers (Kontos & Dunn, 1989). Taken together, these results indicate that providers' attitudes towards parents may be an important determining factor in the quality of parent-provider communication and relationships, and in turn, in parents' experiences with child care.

Other research has documented correlates of parent-provider relationships, including hours in care and parental involvement. Elicker, Noppe, Noppe, and Fortner-Wood (1997) found that parents rated their relationships with providers more favorably when their children were in care more hours per week and when their overall satisfaction with the care was higher. Endsley, Minish, and Zhou (1993) found that the quality of parent-provider communication was associated with greater parental involvement in preschool classrooms.

Parents' experiences with child care, in turn, may affect their children's development (Endsley et al., 1993; Shpancer, 1997). More specifically, van Ijzendoorn, Tavecchio, Stams and Verhoeven (1998) found that the quality of parent-provider communication was related to children's well-being in child care centers. Smith and Hubbard (1988) found similar results, namely, that reciprocal, warm, and balanced parent-provider relationships were associated with better child adjustment at arrival times. In another study, children of mothers who were highly regarded by child care providers performed better on some measures of intellectual and language development (Kontos & Dunn, 1989).

Positive parent-provider relationships may be one component of positive relationships within the parent-provider-child network. For example, Owen et al. (2000) found that both caregiver and mother partnership behavior, including greater communication, were significant predictors of more sensitive and supportive caregiver-child interactions. Ware, Dominique, and Owen (1997 as cited in Shpancer, 1997) also found that higher rates of information exchange between parents and providers were associated with more sensitive caregiving and higher levels of provider involvement with children. While many of the studies are correlational in nature, they suggest that warm and reciprocal relationships between parents and providers are linked with more favorable provider-child interactions, including more verbal interaction, more positive affect, and more supportive discipline (Hogan, Ispa, & Thornburg, 1991; Smith & Hubbard, 1988). Moreover, there may be "spillover" from these positive relationships to children's peer interactions (Churchill, 2003; Hogan et al., 1991). For example, Smith and Hubbard (1988) found that children whose parents had more balanced relationships with providers had more positive social interactions with their peers.

While this research documents positive associations between the quality of parent-provider relationships and children's and families' experiences in child care, other studies fail to provide support for these links. For example, Hogan et al. (1991) found that there were no differences in provider affect, warmth, encouragement, or frequency of conversation with children that could be related to the amount of interaction that took place between parents and providers. Furthermore, interview and observational data may fail to provide consistent results (Endsley et al., 1993; Ghazvini & Readdick, 1994). In fact, Kontos and Wells (1986) suggested that providers might compensate for negative parent-child relationships. More specifically, they found that teachers engaged in more social talk with children whose parents they felt were *not* doing a good job of parenting.

This research, then, supports the importance of parent-provider relationships in early care and education; however, communication between parents and providers remains a challenge. In general, conversations between parents and providers tend to be infrequent and brief (Clarke-Stewart, 1991; Endsley & Minish, 1991; Leavitt, 1995; Zigler & Turner, 1982) though they may be positive and substantive in nature (Shpancer, 1999). According to an ecological framework, the lack of extended communication between parents and providers may hamper young children's development and experiences in child care.

The current study was designed to explore the effects of an intervention meant to improve the quality of relationships and communication between child care providers and parents. The Touchpoints Early Care and Education Initiative involves an intensive 16-hour group training for early care and education providers, focusing on "expanding professionals' repertoires of respectful, collaborative, and strengths-oriented strategies for working with parents and on increasing child care providers' knowledge of child, parent, and family development" (Easterbrooks, Copeman, Goldberg, Miranda, & Swartz, 2007). The purpose of this study was to examine:

(a) whether the intervention, as intended, enhanced the quality of parent-provider relationships and communication as perceived by parents (Hypothesis 1), and (b) whether characteristics of providers and families, were associated with change in these perceptions. More specifically, we expected more favorable change when parents remained with the same providers at Time 1 and Time 2 than when they did not (Hypothesis 2). In addition, we examined whether parental education, child's age, and weekly hours in child care were associated with change in parents' perceptions of their relationships and communication with providers. Based on previous research, we expected that parents of children who were in care for more hours per week may be more satisfied with their communication and view their relationships with providers more positively than parents of children who were in care for fewer hours per week. While we did not have specific hypotheses regarding parental education and child's age, we included these variables in the analysis because of their extensive use throughout the early care and education literature.

Method

Participants

Participants were 94 parents whose young children were enrolled in 14 child care centers. All centers were private child care centers based in a large metropolitan area in the Northeast United States. Centers were located in communities that represented a range of socioeconomic statuses. They ranged in size from a center with 3 infant-toddler classrooms to a center serving children 6 weeks to 6 years with 10 infant-toddler classrooms. Data were collected in infant-toddler classrooms only. Eight centers comprised the intervention group who received the Touchpoints Early Care and Education training; the comparison group was comprised of six centers. Comparison child care centers were meant to receive the intervention following study completion. The intervention group included 49 parents and 36 providers; the comparison group included 45 parents and 38 providers. Forty parents remained with the same caregivers from Time 1 to Time 2 since their children did not transition to different classrooms during the course of the study.

Parents were recruited through letters distributed by center directors and by flyers posted in the centers. Respondents were primarily mothers. Tables 1 and 2 present demographic information for parents and providers. Providers ranged in age from 21 to 59 years ($M = 38.91$ years). All but one of the caregivers were women. Caregivers' experience working as child care providers ranged from less than one year to 38 years ($M = 9.31$ years).

Analyses examining differences between the intervention and comparison groups on parent and provider characteristics showed that parents in intervention sites were more likely to report moderate incomes (\$31,000-\$70,000; adjusted residual = 2.8), while parents in the comparison sites were more likely to report higher incomes (>\$70,000; adjusted residual = 3.8), χ^2 (3, $N = 91$) = 18.73, $p < .01$.

Table 1
Parent Characteristics: Percentages (Frequencies)

	Intervention	Comparison	Overall
	(n = 49)	(n = 45)	(n = 94)
Race/Ethnicity			
Black	30.6 (15)	24.4 (11)	27.7 (26)
White	32.7 (16)	53.3 (24)	42.6 (40)
Hispanic	30.6 (15)	24.4 (11)	27.7 (26)
Other	10.2 (5)	6.7 (3)	8.4 (8)
Education			
Some high school	10.2 (5)	13.3 (6)	11.7 (11)
High school diploma/GED	24.5 (12)	17.8 (8)	21.3 (20)
Some college	30.6 (15)	15.6 (7)	23.4 (22)
B.A./B.S.	6.5 (13)	22.2 (10)	24.5 (23)
Graduate Degree	8.2 (4)	31.1 (14)	19.1 (18)
Income			
Very low (0-15k)	26.5 (13)	20.0 (9)	23.4 (22)
Low (16-30k)	42.9 (21)	28.9 (13)	36.2 (34)
Moderate (31-70k)	16.3 (8)	0.0	8.5 (8)
High (>70k)	12.2 (6)	46.7 (21)	28.7 (27)
Missing Data	2.0 (1)	4.4 (2)	3.2 (3)
Caregiver the same as T1 and T2?			
No	51.0 (25)	64.4 (29)	57.4 (54)
Yes	49.0 (24)	35.6 (16)	42.6 (40)

Parents in comparison sites were more likely to report having a graduate degree (adjusted residual = 2.8), $\chi^2(4, N = 94) = 9.59, p < .05$. Intervention sites had more Asian providers (adjusted residual = 2.3), while comparison sites had more Caucasian providers (adjusted residual = 3.1), $\chi^2 (5, N = 67) = 16.30, p < .01$. Providers at intervention sites were older ($M = 42.21; SD = 10.14$) than providers at comparison sites ($M = 35.39; SD = 10.56$), $t(62) = 2.64, p < .05$.

Table 2
Caregiver Characteristics: Percentages (Frequencies)

	Intervention	Comparison	Overall
	(n = 36)	(n = 38)	(n = 74)
Race/Ethnicity			
Black	36.1 (13)	15.8 (6)	25.7 (19)
White	5.6 (2)	31.6 (12)	18.9 (14)
Hispanic	27.8 (10)	34.2 (13)	31.1 (23)
Other	25.0 (9)	5.2 (2)	14.9 (11)
Missing Data	5.5 (2)	13.2 (5)	9.4 (7)
Education			
Some high school	8.3 (3)	5.3 (2)	6.8 (5)
High school diploma/GED	19.4 (7)	21.1 (8)	20.3 (15)
Some college	47.2 (17)	47.4 (18)	47.3 (35)
Graduated College	19.4 (7)	15.8 (6)	17.6 (13)
Graduate Degree	0.0	0.0	0.0
Missing Data	5.6 (2)	10.5 (4)	8.1 (6)

Note. Demographic data are complete only for caregivers who participated at Time 1.

Measures

A modified version of the Parent-Caregiver Partnership Scale (PCPS; Ware, Barfoot, Rusher, & Owen, 1995) was used to examine changes in parents' perceptions of communication with their child's child care provider. The modified version contains 14 items (compared to 16 items in the original version) to assess the frequency (1 = "Never" to 5 = "Frequently") of information exchange between parent and caregiver (e.g., "How often do you discuss with this caregiver what makes your child angry, sad, or frustrated?" "How often do you receive child development information from this caregiver?" "When your child is having problems at home, how often do you discuss them with this caregiver?"). Selection of items reflected the strengths-based approach of the intervention. The modified version focused on assessing parents' perceptions of their own partnership behavior (9 items) as well as the frequency of caregiver communication (5 items). The original 16-item measure was used in the National Institute of Child Health and Human Development (NICHD) study of Early Child Care and demonstrated good internal consistency (*alpha* = .86 in current study).

The Parent-Caregiver Relationship Scale (PCRS; Elicker et al., 1997) assesses the parent's view of their relationship with their child's caregiver (e.g., "This caregiver is someone you can rely on," "You admire the way this caregiver cares for your child," "This caregiver asks for and values your opinions/advice about this child"). Items are measured on 5-point scales (1 = "Strongly disagree," 5 = "Strongly agree"). A modified version including 14 items was used in this study. Items chosen were consistent with the content of the intervention in order to reflect a strengths-based approach. The measure shows good test-retest reliability (ranging from .69-.71) (Litwin, 1995) and internal consistency (*alpha* = .94 in current study).

The Child Care Experiences Questionnaire was developed by the evaluation team. Three items from this survey were used to create a communication satisfaction composite variable in this study. The first item, satisfaction with communication, was based on an item that asked parents: "How do you feel about the communication between you and your child care provider about this child?" (1 = "Completely satisfied", 4 = "Not at all satisfied"). Second, communication mode match was calculated by considering two additional items on the Child Care Experiences Questionnaire. The first was "What methods of communication do your child care providers use with you?" The second question was "What methods of communication do you prefer?" Parents were asked to check off as many of the following that applied: phone calls, parent-teacher conferences, face-to-face at drop-off and pick-up, bulletin boards, and notes. Communication mode match was calculated simply by counting the number of matches between modes that the parent preferred and modes they said that caregivers used. The communication satisfaction composite variable used in this analysis was created by first recoding the communication satisfaction item so that higher was better, and then averaging the z-scores of communication satisfaction and communication mode match.

Procedures

Intervention. Providers in the intervention sites received the Touchpoints Early Care and Education training, a developmental and relationship-based training aimed at enhancing provider-parent relationships and communication. Providers attended the 16-hour trainings (over 2 or 3 sessions) with center co-workers and directors. Training was provided by two trained facilitators using case vignettes, presentations, parent quotes, videotaped encounters, and interactive exercises (Brazelton Touchpoints Center, n.d.). More specifically, the trainings included:

> [a presentation] of the Touchpoints™ Developmental and Relational Frameworks, particularly the elements of parent-child-provider relationships in the first six years of a child's life…and [a discussion of] how the Touchpoints™ approach can be used to benefit the child, the parents, and the educator (e.g. how early childhood educators can use the Touchpoints™ approach to help

parents deepen their understanding of a child's behavior and establish a more successful system of relationships for all involved)
(Brazelton Touchpoints Center, n.d.).

Data Collection. A pre-test/post-test comparison design was used to assess key
constructs at baseline (pre-intervention, T1) and approximately 6 months post-intervention (T2). This design allowed for the analysis of change over time and inter-
vention/comparison group differences in parents' perceptions of their relationships
and communication with caregivers. At both times, questionnaire packets were
distributed to parents in intervention and comparison sites by center directors.

Results

Analyses addressed several research questions aimed at understanding the effects
of the intervention. First, we expected that parents in the intervention group would
report greater positive change in their perceptions of their relationships (measured by
the PCRS) and communication (measured by the PCPS and report of "satisfaction
with communication") with child care providers than would parents in the comparison group (Hypothesis 1). In addition, we explored whether characteristics of providers and families would influence these results. More specifically, we expected more
favorable change when parents remained with the same caregiver at Time 1 and Time
2 than when they did not (Hypothesis 2). In addition, we examined whether parental
education, child age, and weekly hours in child care might influence these results.

Three standard linear regressions, one on each of the change scores for the
three outcome variables (PCRS, PCPS, and composite communication satisfaction
variable) were conducted. This method of analysis allowed us to simultaneously
examine both research questions, and the effects of both continuous and categori-
cal variables of interest. Change scores were calculated by subtracting Time 1 from
Time 2 scores for each variable.

Descriptive Statistics

Table 3 shows descriptive statistics for all continuous variables for the whole
sample as well as for the intervention and comparison groups.

Bivariate Analysis

Correlations between all continuous predictor and outcomes variables are presented in the Appendix (pp. 72-73). Highest education and income were highly correlated ($r = .73, p < .01$) thus income was dropped from the analysis. Highest education
was also significantly negatively correlated with change in PCRS scores and communication mode matches at Time 1. As might be expected, Time 1 and Time 2 scores

Table 3
Variable Means

Variable	Intervention	Comparison	Overall
	(n = 49)	(n = 45)	(n = 94)
Hours per week in care	38.92	39.31	39.05
Child Age (in months at Time 1)	17.61	15.69	16.45
PCRS T1	4.21	4.56	4.38
PCRS T2	4.38	4.39	4.39
PCPS T1	3.39	3.65	3.52
PCPS T2	3.55	3.73	3.64
Satisfaction with Communication T1	1.56	1.43	1.50
Satisfaction with Communication T2	1.56	1.55	1.55
Communication Mode MatchesT1	4.23	4.16	4.20
Communication Mode Matches T2	4.08	4.11	4.07

Note. PCRS = Parent-Caregiver Relationship Scale; PCPS = Parent-Caregiver Partnership Scale

for each variable were moderately correlated. PCPS and PCRS scores were also moderately correlated both at Time 1 and Time 2, and were negatively correlated with communication satisfaction scores, indicating that when relationships and communication were better (lower scores), parents were more satisfied with communication. Change scores for PCRS and PCPS were also positively correlated, and PCRS change scores were positively correlated with change in the communication satisfaction composite variable. Finally, change scores for all three outcome variables were negatively correlated with their respective Time 1 scores, suggesting a ceiling effect.

Regression Results

A series of regression models was run to test the relations between the predictor variables of interest (site type, caregiver match, parent's highest education, hours per week in child care, child age at Time 1) and change scores for each outcome variable, PCRS, PCPS, and composite communication satisfaction. In each regression, we controlled for Time 1 scores and race/ethnicity using three dummy variables (Black vs. Not Black, White vs. Not White, Hispanic vs. Not Hispanic). We also tested two-way interactions between variables of interest for each set of regression models.

PCRS regression results. Control variables (PCRS Time 1 scores and race/ethnicity) were entered as a block, followed by site type, caregiver match, highest education, hours per week, and child's age at Time 1. Two-way interactions of interest were then entered as a block. These included: Site Type X Caregiver Match, Site Type X Highest Education, Site Type X Hours per week, Site Type X Child Age, Caregiver Match X Child Age, and Caregiver Match X Hours per week.

Results are summarized in Table 4. In the best fitting model, multiple R for the regression was statistically significant, $F(8, 83) = 9.36, p < .001, R^2 = .48$. Four of the independent variables (PCRS Time 1 scores, site type, caregiver match, and highest education) contributed significantly to the prediction of change in PCRS scores ($p < .01$). PCRS Time 1 scores were negatively correlated with change in PCRS scores, most likely illustrating a ceiling effect. Caregiver match was positively correlated with PCRS change scores, indicating that when parents reported on the same caregivers at Time 1 and Time 2 there was more improvement in their PCRS scores than when they reported on different caregivers. Both site type and highest education were negatively correlated with PCRS change scores. The interaction between site type and highest education was also significant.

Table 4

Standard Regression Analysis Summary for Variables Predicting Change in Parent-Caregiver Relationship (PCRS) Scores

Variable	B	SEB	β
PCRS T1	-.08***	.01	-.54
Black (1) /Non-Black (0)	.01	.22	.005
White (1) /Non-White (0)	.11	.20	.09
Hispanic (1) /Non-Hispanic (0)	.30	.22	.21
Site Type (1 = intervention, 2 = comparison)	-.87**	.29	-.67
Caregiver Match (0 = No, 1 = Yes)	.34**	.11	.26
Highest Education	-.43**	.15	-.85
Site Type x Highest Education	.25**	.09	1.11

Note. R^2 = .48 (N = 92, p < .001)
*$p < .05$;** $p < .01$; *** $p < .001$

Figure 1 shows a "prototypical" plot illustrating the interaction based on the current data. As the plot illustrates, parents in the intervention group who were less educated reported more improvement in their relationships with caregivers than did parents who were more highly educated. However, this effect did not hold for parents in the comparison group. Parents in the comparison group who were less educated seemed to report slightly less positive change in their relationships than

Figure 1
Prototypical Plot for Site Type X Highest Education Interaction

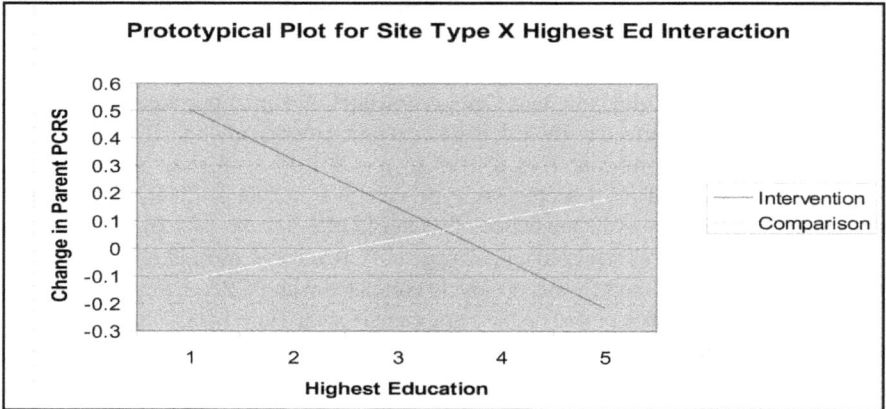

parents who were more highly educated. Finally, while all of the race/ethnicity dummy variables were positively correlated with change in PCRS scores, none of them made a statistically significant contribution to the prediction of change in PCRS scores.

PCPS regression results. Control variables (PCPS Time 1 scores and race/ethnicity) were entered as a block, followed by site type, caregiver match, highest education, hours per week, and child age at Time 1. The same two-way interactions that were tested for the PCRS analysis were entered as a block.

Results are summarized in Table 5. In the best fitting model, multiple R for the regression was statistically significant, $F (4, 87) = 8.49$, $p < .001$, $R^2 = .28$. Only PCPS Time 1 scores contributed significantly to the prediction of change in PCPS scores ($p < .001$). PCPS Time 1 scores were negatively correlated with change in PCPS scores. Two of the race/ethnicity dummy variables were positively correlated with change in PCPS scores, and one was negatively correlated. However, none of the race/ethnicity dummy variables made a statistically significant contribution to the prediction of change in PCPS scores ($p > .05$). None of the other variables of interest or interactions contributed significantly to the prediction of change in PCPS Scores.

Composite communication satisfaction regression results. Control variables (composite communication satisfaction Time 1 scores and race/ethnicity) were entered as a block, followed by site type, caregiver match, highest education, hours per week, and child age at Time 1. The same two-way interactions that were tested for PCRS and PCPS analyses were entered as a block in this analysis.

Table 5
Standard Regression Analysis Summary for Variables Predicting Change in Parent-Caregiver Partnership (PCPS) Scores

Variable	B	SEB	β
PCPS T1	-.44***	.09	-.47
Black (1) /Non-Black (0)	.02	.27	.01
White (1) /Non-White (0)	-.25	.25	-.18
Hispanic (1) /Non-Hispanic (0)	.32	.25	.20

Note. $R^2 = .28$ ($N = 92, p < .001$)
***$p < .001$

Results are summarized in Table 6. In the best fitting model, multiple R for the regression was statistically significant, $F (5, 86) = 8.62, p < .001, R^2 = .33$. Two of the independent variables, T1 scores and caregiver match, contributed significantly to the prediction of change in composite communication satisfaction scores. Time 1 scores were negatively correlated with change scores. Caregiver match was positively correlated, indicating that when parents reported on the same caregivers at Time 1 and Time 2, there was more improvement in their satisfaction with communication than when they reported on different caregivers. Finally, while all of the race/ethnicity dummy variables were positively correlated with change in communication satisfaction composite scores, none of them made a statistically significant contribution to the prediction of change in these scores (p > .05). None of the other variables of interest or interactions contributed significantly to the prediction of change in communication satisfaction scores.

Table 6
Standard Regression Analysis Summary for Variables Predicting Change in Composite Communication Satisfaction Scores

Variable	B	SEB	β
Composite Communication Satisfaction T1	-.60***	.11	-.53
Black (1) /Non-Black (0)	.07	.31	.03
White (1) /Non-White (0)	.50	.30	.28
Hispanic (1) /Non-Hispanic (0)	.43	.30	.22
Caregiver Match	.38*	.17	.22

Note. $R^2 = .33$ ($N = 92, p < .001$)
*$p < .05$; *** $p < .001$

Discussion

The primary aim of this study was to examine the effectiveness of an intervention designed to enhance relationships and communication between parents and child care providers. The results indicated that the intervention was, in fact, successful in improving parents' perceptions of their relationships with their children's child care providers. Another aim of the study was to consider whether characteristics of families and providers were associated with changes in parents' perceptions of relationships and communication. Specifically, we expected that parents' perceptions would improve more if they stayed with the same caregiver across the 6 months of the study than if they did not. This hypothesis also was supported.

The fact that the intervention led to positive changes in parents' perceptions of their relationships with providers is not surprising. As opposed to prescriptive or top-down approaches to working with families, the intervention emphasized a collaborative approach to relationships with parents and the importance of valuing those relationships. The items that parents were asked to consider on the Parent-Caregiver Relationship Scale (PCRS) address constructs such as trust, respect, admiration, and collaboration – the very aspects of relationships that this particular intervention was designed to promote.

The intervention, however, did not have consistent effects across parents of all education levels. The interaction effect between site type (intervention vs. comparison) and education level showed that the intervention seemed to produce more positive changes for parents with less education than for parents with more education. Those parents who were less educated also came from lower socioeconomic backgrounds. It is possible that the nature of the intervention, and its emphasis on valuing parents' strengths, played an especially important role for parents who may not feel as empowered in other aspects of their lives. This question certainly merits further exploration. These results validate the need to examine how an intervention or prevention program might be differentially effective depending on characteristics of child care providers, the families they serve, and the contexts in which these programs are implemented.

Parents' perceptions of relationships improved in the intervention group; however, participation in the intervention did not predict change in parents' perceptions of frequency of communication, as measured by the PCPS, nor in their satisfaction with communication with providers. The fact that the intervention did not lead to changes in parents' perceptions of communication may simply be a reflection of the challenges associated with parent-provider communication in child care centers. Communication between parents and providers in such settings generally tends to be brief and infrequent (Clarke-Stewart, 1991; Endsley & Minish, 1991; Leavitt, 1995; Zigler & Turner, 1982). Despite the fact that providers participated in this training meant to improve parent-provider communication, they are still constrained by the everyday challenges of working in child care centers, including rushed pick-up and drop-off times and the resulting lack of time to talk with parents. Thus, although parents were more satisfied with their relationships post-intervention than they were pre-intervention, they still may like to have more opportunities to communicate with their children's child care providers.

Furthermore, while communication may be an important aspect of relationships, perhaps it is not the frequency of communication that matters most for parents, but rather the tone and content that are most important. Even when communication occurs frequently, it is possible that the way in which providers talk with parents may be negative or unsupportive. This could potentially leave parents feeling devalued and disempowered. The primary purpose of this intervention was not to increase frequency of communication, but rather to encourage providers to value their relationships with parents, and through their communication, to show their respect and trust in parents' strengths and parenting abilities. The fact that the intervention did improve relationships, but not communication, could indicate that in the limited time that providers do spend talking with parents, they are better able to help parents feel valued and respected.

The other notable variable of interest in this study was "caregiver match" – whether or not the parent reported on the same provider across time. Research shows that providers and parents who stay together longer may have opportunities to build stronger relationships (Essa et al., 1999). In fact, this study showed that parents who reported on the same caregiver at Time 1 and Time 2 were more likely to improve in their perceptions of their relationships when compared with parents who reported on different caregivers.

Caregiver match also contributed significantly to the prediction of change in parents' satisfaction with communication with their providers. Parents' satisfaction with communication improved more when they remained with the same caregiver from Time 1 to Time 2 than when they did not. Caregiver match, however, did not predict change in parents' perceptions of the frequency of communication that took place between parents and providers. Perhaps staying with the same provider helps parents and providers get to know each other better, and as a result, despite the limited time they may have to communicate, parents may become increasingly comfortable with the communication styles of providers. In addition, as providers get to know parents, they may become more effective at conveying meaningful and helpful information in supportive ways in the limited time that they have to communicate.

Conclusions and Implications for Practice

Overall, this intervention was effective in improving relationships between parents and providers, especially for parents with less education or lower income. Training and other professional development opportunities that focus not only on increasing communication with parents, but on valuing relationships with parents, have the potential to play an important role in families' experiences with child care.

Furthermore, continuity of care was an important factor in parent-provider re-lationships and parents' satisfaction with communication. While some child care centers practice continuity of care (or looping), many do not (Essa et al., 1999; Hegde & Cassidy, 2004). In many centers, children either "age out" of a classroom or are moved up when they achieve certain developmental milestones, such as walk-ing. In light of these results, perhaps more programs should consider implementing continuity of care. Unfortunately, when centers do have continuity of care policies, teacher turnover remains high, thus posing a challenge to successfully putting these policies into practice (Shonkoff & Phillips, 2000). The field needs to continue to work to find creative and successful ways of attracting and retaining high quality teachers in order to provide opportunities for parents and providers to build consis-tent and stable relationships.

Our findings suggest that continuity of care and training that is meant to en-hance provider-parent relationships foster stronger bonds between parents and the providers who care for their young children. Consistency and stability in relation-ships and in-service teacher training are already seen as important aspects of quality in early care and education settings (Harms, Cryer & Clifford, 2003; Shonkoff & Phillips, 2000). The results of this study further emphasize the importance of these components for parent-provider relationships, and in turn, high quality early care and education.

Future Directions

This study has several implications for future research. First, results indicate that relationship-based training can lead to positive outcomes, at least from parents' per-spectives. Future research could shed light on whether such training has similar ef-fects on providers' views of relationships. Second, some research has already shown a connection between parent-provider relationships and the ways in which teachers and children interact (Owen et al., 2000; Smith & Hubbard, 1988; van Ijzendoorn et al., 1998). Further research might explore the effects of relationship-based interventions for children's experiences in child care. Finally, while frequency of communication is certainly a potentially important factor in parent-provider relationships and quality of care, future research could also examine more closely how relationship-based inter-ventions may affect the tone and content of communication that takes place between parents and providers in early care and education settings.

References

Barnas, M. V., & Cummings, E. M. (1994). Caregiver stability and toddlers' attachment-related behavior towards caregivers in day care. *Infant Behavior & Development, 17*, 141-147.
Brazelton Touchpoints Center. (n.d.). Touchpoints early care and education

training program. *Touchpoints*. Retrieved February 11, 2007, from http://www.touchpoints.org/ecet.html.

Bronfenbrenner, U. (2001). Ecological models of human development. In M. Gauvain & M. Cole (Eds.), *Readings on the development of children (3rd ed.)* (pp. 3-8). New York: Worth Publishers.

Burchinal, M. R., Roberts, J. E., Riggins, R., Zeisel, S. A., Neebe, E., & Bryant, D. (2000). Relating quality of center-based child care to early cognitive and language development longitudinally. *Child Development, 71*, 339-357.

Churchill, S. L. (2003). Goodness-of-fit in early childhood settings. *Early Childhood Education Journal, 31(2),* 113-117.

Clarke-Stewart, K. A. (1991). A home is not a school: The effects of child care on children's development. *Journal of Social Issues, 47*, 105–123.

Easterbrooks, A., Copeman, A., Goldberg, J. L., Miranda, C., & Swartz, M. I. (2007, March). *Supporting parent-provider relationships in early child care and education.* Paper presented at the Society for Research in Child Development, Boston, MA.

Elicker, J., Noppe, I. C., Noppe, L. D., & Fortner-Wood, C. (1997). The parent-caregiver relationship scale: Rounding out the relationship system in infant child care. *Early Education and Development, 8(1),* 83-100.

Endsley, R. C., & Minish, P. A. (1991). Parent-staff communication in day care centers during morning and afternoon transitions. *Early Childhood Research Quarterly, 6,* 119-135.

Endsley, R. C., Minish, P. A., & Zhou, Q. (1993). Parent involvement and quality day care in proprietary centers. *Journal of Research in Childhood Education, 7(2),* 53-61.

Essa, E. L., Favre, K., Thweatt, G., & Waugh, S. (1999). Continuity of care for infants and toddlers. *Early Child Development and Care, 148*, 11-19.

Ghazvini, A. S., & Readdick, C. A. (1994). Parent-caregiver communication and quality of care in diverse child care settings. *Early Childhood Research Quarterly, 9,* 207-242.

Hamre, B. K., & Pianta, R. C. (2001). Self-reported depression in non-familial caregivers: Prevalence and associations with caregiver behavior in child-care settings. *Early Childhood Research Quarterly, 19*, 297-318.

Harms, T., Cryer, D., & Clifford, R. M. (2003). *Infant/Toddler Environment Rating Scale-Revised.* New York: Teachers College Press.

Hegde, A. V., & Cassidy, D. J. (2004). Teacher and parent perspectives on looping. *Early Childhood Education Journal, 32,* 133-138.

Hofferth, S., Shauman, K., Henke, R., & West, J. (1998). *Characteristics of children's early care and education programs:Data from the 1995 National Household Education Survey (NCES 98-128).* Washington, DC: U.S. Government Printing Office.

Hogan, E., Ispa, J. M., & Thornburg, K. R. (1991). Mother-provider interaction and the provider-child relationship in family child care homes. *Early Child Development and Care, 77*, 57-65.

Howes, C. (1988). Relations between early child care and schooling. *Developmental Psychology, 24*, 53-57.

Howes, C., & Hamilton C. E. (1992). Children's relationships with child care teachers: Stability and concordance with parental attachments. *Child Development, 63*, 867-878.

Howes, C., Hamilton, C. E., & Matheson, C. C. (1994). Children's relationships with peers: Differential associations with aspects of the teacher-child relationship. *Child Development, 65*, 253-263.

Howes, C., Matheson, C. C., & Hamilton, C. E. (1994). Maternal, teacher, and child care history correlates of children's relationships with peers. *Child Development, 65*, 264-273.

Kontos, S., & Dunn, L. (1989). Attitudes of caregivers, maternal experiences with day care, and children's development. *Journal of Applied Developmental Psychology, 10*, 37-51.

Kontos, S., & Wells, W. (1986). Attitudes of caregivers and the day care experiences of families. *Early Childhood Research Quarterly, 1*, 47-67.

Leavitt, R. L. (1995). Parent-provider communication in family day care homes. *Child and Youth Care Forum, 24(4)*, 231- 245.

Litwin, M. S. (1995). *How to measure survey reliability and validity.* Thousand Oaks, CA: Sage Publications.

Owen, M. T., Ware, A. M., & Barfoot, B. (2000). Caregiver-mother partnership behavior and the quality of caregiver-child and mother-child interactions. *Early Childhood Research Quarterly, 15(3)*, 413-428.

Pianta, R. C., & Stuhlman, M. W. (2004). Teacher-child relationships and children's success in the first years of school. *School Psychology Review, 33*, 444-458.

Powell, D. R. (1997). Parents' contributions to the quality of child care arrangements. *Advances in Early Education and Day Care, 9*, 133-155.

Shonkoff, J. P., & Phillips, D. (2000). *From neurons to neighborhoods: The science of early development.* Committee on Integrating the Science of Early Childhood Development. Washington, DC: National Academy Press.

Shpancer, N. (1997). The link between caregiver-parent relations and children's experiences in day care and at home: What does the research tell us? *Early Child Development and Care, 135*, 7-20.

Shpancer, N. (1999). Caregiver-parent relations in daycare: Testing the buffer hypothesis. *Early Child Development and Care, 156*, 1-14.

Smith, A. B., & Hubbard, P. M. (1988). The relationship between parent/staff communication and children's behavior in early childhood settings. *Early Child Development and Care, 35*, 13-28.

Sroufe, L. A., Egeland, B., Carlson, E. A., & Collins, W. A. (2005). *The development of the person: The Minnesota Study of Risk and Adaptation from Birth to Adulthood.* New York: Guilford Press.

Thompson, R. A. (1999). Early attachment and later development. In J. Cassidy & P. R. Shaver (Eds.), *Handbook of attachment: Theory, research and clinical applications* (pp. 265-286). New York: Guilford Press.

U.S. Department of Education, National Center for Education Statistics. (2006). *Digest of Education Statistics, 2005* (NCES 2006–030).

van Ijzendoorn, M. H., Tavecchio, L. W. C., Stams, G., & Verhoeven, E. R. (1998). Attunement between parents and professional caregivers: A Comparison of childrearing attitudes in different child-care settings. *Journal of Marriage and the Family, 60(3),* 771-781.

Ware, A. M., Barfoot, B., Rusher, A. S., & Owen, M. T. (1995, March). *The caregiver role in the parent-caregiver partnership: Its relationship to the child care environment.* Poster presented at the Biennial Meeting of the Society for Research in Child Development, Indianapolis, IN.

Ware, A. M., Dominque, G. C., & Owen, M. T. (1997, April). *Predicting variation in parent-caregiver partnership behaviors.* Paper presented at the Biennial Meeting of the Society for Research in Child Development, Washington DC.

Whitebook, M., Sakai, L. M., & Howes, C. (2004). Improving and sustaining center quality: The role of NAEYC accreditation and staff stability. *Early Education & Development, 15,* 305-325.

Zigler, E. F., & Turner, P. (1982). Parents and day care workers: A failed partnership? In E. F. Zigler & E. W. Gordon (Eds.), *Day care: Scientific and social policy issues* (pp. 174-182). Boston: Auburn House.

Appendix
Correlations (N = 94).

Variables	1	2	3	4	5	6	7
1. Child Age (T1)	--	--	--	--	--	--	--
2. Highest Education	-.14	--	--	--	--	--	--
3. Hours per week	-.07	.08	--	--	--	--	--
4. Income	-.15	.73**	.13	--	--	--	--
5. PCPS T1	-.17	-.03	.04	-.04	--	--	--
6. PCPS T2	-.19	-.18	.08	-.18	.59**	--	--
7. PCRS T1	-.12	.05	.02	.09	.58**	.40**	--
8. PCRS T2	-.05	-.15	.10	-.10	.35**	.59**	.37**
9. Change PCPS (T2 – T1)	-.04	-.18	.05	-.16	-.40**	.51**	-.17
10. Change PCRS (T2 – T1)	.12	-.22*	.10	-.18	-.18	.20	-.56**
11. Comm Satisfaction T1	.06	.02	-.03	.02	-.32**	-.31**	-.46**
12. Comm Satisfaction T2	-.01	.01	-.11	.02	-.23*	-.41**	-.29**
13. Comm Mode Matches T1	-.10	-.26*	-.10	-.36**	.08	.18	.04
14. Comm Mode Matches T2	.19	-.05	-.16	-.19	-.08	.13	.06
15. Composite Comm Sat T1	-.11	-.19	-.05	-.25*	.27**	.33**	.33**
16. Composite Comm Sat T2	.11	-.04	-.03	-.12	.09	.33**	.22*
17. Change Comp Comm Sat	.20	.14	.02	.12	-.15	.02	-.08

*p < .05; **p < .01

Appendix
Correlations (N = 94).

8	9	10	11	12	13	14	15	16
--	--	--	--	--	--	--	--	--
--	--	--	--	--	--	--	--	--
--	--	--	--	--	--	--	--	--
--	--	--	--	--	--	--	--	--
--	--	--	--	--	--	--	--	--
--	--	--	--	--	--	--	--	--
--	--	--	--	--	--	--	--	--
--	--	--	--	--	--	--	--	--
.28**	--	--	--	--	--	--	--	--
.57**	.39**	--	--	--	--	--	--	--
-.20	-.01	.19	--	--	--	--	--	--
-.45**	-.22*	-.20	.33**	--	--	--	--	--
.12	.12	.07	-.12	-.16	--	--	--	--
.16	.23*	.08	-.06	-.27**	.42**	--	--	--
.22*	.09	-.07	-.74**	-.32**	.75**	.32**	--	--
.36**	.28**	.16	-.22*	-.79**	.37*	.80**	.40**	--
.16	.19	.22*	.44**	-.46**	-.31**	.48**	-.50**	.59**

Emotional Availability and the Complexity of Child Care: A Commentary

Ora Aviezer
Oranim Academic College of Education and University of Haifa, Israel

Changing perceptions about young children's needs have led to emphasizing relationships between children and their child-care providers and their added significance as markers of quality of care, mostly in the family, but also in group settings (Rutter & O'Connor, 1999). Congruent with this emphasis, the papers in this mini-series focused on relationships within the context of non-maternal child care and their direct and indirect influences on children's development as well as on the quality of their care. Shivers' review points to links of care provider's professional educational experiences as well as perceived economic well-being and child-rearing beliefs to emotional availability and makes a convincing argument for the usefulness of evaluating emotional availability in various child care contexts. Biringen et al. describe how Emotional Availability Scales (EAS) and Attachment Q-set (AQS), which are dyadic measures, can be adapted for a group setting and be used successfully in an intervention program designed to improve providers' and children's emotional availability. Swartz and Easterbrooks describe an intervention designed to enhance relationships and communication between parents and providers as another aspect of quality care. Finally, Howes and Hong examine emotional availability at home and at child care for children of Mexican-heritage and how it contributes to their social competence in pre-kindergarten.

According to the ecological theory of development (Bronfenbrenner, 1989), child-provider relationships are embedded within a system of multiple contexts, which include additional relationships and events that directly and indirectly affect the child within a broader social context. Thus, the complexity of children's environments needs to be considered in order to identify the determining factors of children's experiences in child care as well as the developmental outcomes. Children who receive non-maternal care, whether individually or in groups, live within a complex context of caretaking ecology which is constituted of at least two quite

All correspondence should be addressed to Ora Aviezer, Center for the Study of Child Development, Rabin Bldg #6035, University of Haifa, Haifa, 31905, Israel. Electronic mail may be sent oaviezer@psy.haifa.ac.il.

different immediate environments. To use the terminology of ecological system's theory (Bronfenbrenner, 1989), within each day these children are involved in two separate microsystems, which are characterized by different patterns of activity and material features, and in which relationships are formed with individuals whose beliefs may be different (van IJzendoorn, Tavecchio, Stams, Verhoeven, & Reiling, 1998). Moreover, interaction between parents and professional care providers (the mesosystem) adds additional complexity to an already complex ecology. Finally, children are affected by more distal processes emanating from the exosystem in which caregivers' own economic and social considerations and concerns are represented and the macrosystem which is the source of ethnic and cultural influences.

Against this complex background of multiple social contexts the influence of providers' style of interaction with children needs to be evaluated. Most of the studies in this mini-series evaluated provider-child interaction by using the Emotional Availability Scales (EAS). Bretherton (2000) argued that despite the different theoretical roots of emotional availability and attachment they share similar underlying assumptions about the importance of sensitive caregiving for good quality care. Emotional availability is founded on mutually rewarding regulation of activities and affective states, such that higher emotional availability scores entail an emotional atmosphere that is marked by positive affect rather than by absence of negative affect. Therefore, the conceptualization of dyadic emotional availability considers maternal sensitivity as only one of its components along with maternal structuring, non-intrusiveness and non-hostility and child's responsiveness and involvement (Easterbrooks & Biringen, 2000).

Based on attachment research it was suggested that maternal sensitivity is an important determinant of attachment security, but not exclusively, because attachment security is particularly liable to environmental influences (Belsky, 1999; De Wolff & van IJzendoorn, 1997). Moderating effects on children's development of attachment security were therefore postulated for child care contexts of low quality. Indeed NICHD (1997) found that children in low quality center care were more strongly affected by their mother's behavior compared to children in high quality care, and a combination of less sensitive and less responsive care by mothers and providers created a risk effect for children's attachment. Quality of care was particularly implicated in two studies in Israel that evaluated attachment security and emotional availability and found higher prevalence of insecure attachment among infants from low quality group care, despite the normative high emotional availability of their mothers (Aviezer, Sagi, Joels, & Ziv, 1999; Aviezer, Sagi-Schwartz, & Koren-Karie, 2003).

The first study (Aviezer et al., 1999) examined the full model of attachment transmission in a small sample of mothers and infants from two kibbutz groups, a collectively sleeping group and a home sleeping group. High quality care in a group setting characterized the two groups during the day. However, the home sleeping group spent the night at home with their families whereas the collective sleeping group spent the night in the children's house away from their parents and were supervised by non-familiar night-watch persons who rotated every week (for details about the kibbutz and its educational practices see Aviezer, van IJzendoorn, Sagi, & Schuengel, 1994). This latter practice provided the children from the collective group with low quality care at night. The two groups were comparable in emotional availability particularly in maternal sensitivity, but higher prevalence of attachment insecurity was found for infants in the collective sleeping group. Moreover, the full model of attachment transmission was operating only in the home sleeping group (i.e., high emotional availability was associated with both maternal autonomous representations and infants' attachment security). Such associations were not found for the collective sleeping group where the likelihood that an autonomous and sensitive mother would raise a secure infant was equal to the likelihood that she would raise an insecure infant. These findings were interpreted to indicate that children's intensive experience of low quality non-maternal care moderates the quality of their relations to their mothers.

To replicate these findings, the same hypothesis was examined in a large urban sample (Aviezer et al., 2003). This study examined the association between maternal sensitivity and infants' secure attachment in two groups: One group of children experienced extensive group care in daycare centers which was characterized by low standards and low emotional quality of care (Koren-Karie, Sagi-Schwartz, & Egoz-Mizrachi, 2005), and a second group of children received individual home care. The two groups were comparable on socioeconomic status (SES) and maternal sensitivity, but the prevalence of insecure attachment was significantly higher in the daycare group. Similar to mothers of collectively sleeping kibbutz infants, in the daycare group the likelihood that a sensitive mother would bring up a secure infant was equal to the likelihood that she would raise an insecure infant. These findings do not contrast Shivers' (this issue) review and conclusion that attachment relationships in child care are important. Rather, they underscore the importance of high quality care for the formation of attachment relations. Based on our studies it is suggested that child care environments which are characterized by intensive low quality of care should be viewed as vulnerable child-care contexts with regards to their influence on children's attachment relations to their mothers.

Concordant with Baron and Kenny (1986), the findings from the Israeli studies suggest that non-maternal care of low quality functioned as a moderator variable by affecting the assumed causal relations between maternal sensitivity and infant attachment security. It appears that in these vulnerable child-care contexts, children's emotional needs tended to get activated but provider's proper attention and care was not provided. Thus, facing an environment of many infants and few providers, infants are bound to feel frustrated and unprotected and to experience their mothers' absence as an indication of maternal inaccessibility and unavailability, which then jeopardizes their sense of being protected by their mothers. In the quality of care of collectively sleeping kibbutz infants (Aviezer et al., 1999) and center care children (Aviezer et al., 2003) there was an inherent inconsistency between their experiences during the day (poor for center children; good for kibbutz children) and their experiences during the night (good for center children; poor for kibbutz children). These discrepant experiences were associated with more attachment insecurity to mother, possibly because children's difficulties that originated in the context of non-maternal care can make their way into the home context and complicate children's relations with mothers. Concordant with the attachment construct, these children seem to respond to their mother's critical absence when they are in need rather than to her sensitivity when she is present.

Although the family and professional care setting constitute two separate environments, children participate actively in both settings and their well-being is affected by their experiences in both of them. Van IJzendoorn et al. (1998) found that discrepant child-rearing attitudes of parents and professional providers were associated with children's lower well-being. They recommended careful matching with regard to child rearing attitudes prior to enrollment and open communication between parents and providers to facilitate continuity between the two microsystems in which the child receives care. However, such prior matching may be unrealistic in many settings and for many parents. Thus, Swartz and Easterbrooks' Touchpoint intervention (this issue), which was found effective for improving parents' perceptions of their relationships with providers is an important step in the direction of creating continuity between the home and the child care center. Moreover, improving parent-provider interaction in an atmosphere of collaboration and mutual valuing might have positive effects similar to the effects of collaborative communication between parents and teachers (Seginer, 2006).

The papers by Howes and Hong (this issue) as well as by Shivers (this issue) remind us of the challenges faced by minority mothers as they need to integrate their children into institutions that represent the dominant culture and the inherent differences that need to be reconciled in such a process. In the face of increasing globalization, it is important to underscore that quality of care in immediate environments is always embedded within more distal cultural contexts which may generate larger discrepancies between immediate environments, and may be manifested in varied beliefs as well as behavior. Roer-Strier and Rosenthal (2001) examined the goals of socialization in the context of immigration and argued that child rearing ideologies and socialization practices are functional and future oriented. They introduced the "adaptive adult" metaphor which reflects parents' ideals for their children's functioning as adults. This metaphor is a dynamic concept that varies across cultures. Thus, parents' image of "adaptive adult" which reflects the culture of the immigrating families or the minority culture is likely to be different from the images of "adaptive adult" which are fostered by the dominant culture. Consequently, given that policies are directed by the dominant culture, children from minority groups are faced with conflicting messages that originate from discrepancies in beliefs and behaviors of parents and providers. Children's success in the dominant culture could benefit considerably by interventions that would foster open communication between minority mothers and their children's providers (such as suggested by Swartz & Easterbrook, this issue). However, these interventions involve additional complexity that derives from interaction between two sets of cultural values.

Such culturally rooted discrepancies are evident in Howes and Hong's (this issue) paper, where the discrepancies are embedded right within the assessment of emotional availability and are manifested in relatively high sensitivity combined with relatively low structuring. In this context it may be useful to reiterate Ward and Carlson's (1995) suggestion that different caregiving contexts might lend different meanings to the construct of maternal sensitivity and raise the question whether the meaning of sensitive mothering and affective play interactions is always the same regardless of the specific ecology in which they are observed. Indeed as Howes and Hong commented, the high maternal sensitivity scores of Latina mothers (also see Shivers in this issue) are a source of maternal strength. However, it is maternal structuring that appears to distinguish care practices in the Latina culture from the dominant American culture. Therefore, a longitudinal follow-up of the trajectory of maternal structuring within the context of the emotional availability construct may be informative about changes in mothers' interactive styles as their children immerse into the dominant culture, and the extent of their adaptation to it. Moreover, in this population, lower sensitivity scores for mothers and providers should not be disregarded as they are likely to represent dyads higher at risk that are poorly equipped with strength from their minority culture when they need to deal with the challenges presented by the dominant culture.

Finally, as noted by Howes (1999), children's experiences in child care are predicted by the quality of the child care environment. Moreover, children get attached to their providers who provide them with regular physical and emotional care, and sensitive child-provider interaction leads to the formation of secure attachment. Thus, improving the quality of care for children would not be feasible unless attention is given to providers and their interaction with children. Educating providers about the central role that relationships in general and attachment in particular play in child development, such as suggested by Biringen and colleagues (Biringen et al., this issue), appears to be a promising intervention strategy. The goal of refining providers' observation skills and facilitating their emotional availability with children in a group setting (Biringen et al., this issue) is particularly commendable and should be useful for improving providers' sensitivity, promoting their professional development, and hence influencing the quality of care they provide as argued by Shivers (this issue). Moreover, investing in providers' emotional availability and facilitating their understanding of relationships in and of itself may ultimately serve to reduce the inherent discrepancy between the two different environments in which children, who receive out of home care, find themselves. There is evidence that structural standards contribute to high quality child care (NICHD, 1996, 2000) and to child outcomes (NICHD, 1999). Consequently, enforcing such standards is viewed as a requirement and it is now time to move forward towards providing quality care to children. This could be accomplished by investing in their relations with their care providers through fostering emotional availability in the relationships between children and providers. This should become the next uncontested contribution to the quality of child care as children will experience high quality relationships in their immediate environment, regardless of whether the particular context of care is the home or non-parental care setting.

References

Aviezer, O., Sagi, A., Joels, T., & Ziv, Y. (1999). Emotional availability and attachment representations in kibbutz infants and their mothers. *Developmental Psychology, 35,* 811-821.

Aviezer, O., Sagi-Schwartz, A., & Koren-Karie, N. (2003). Ecological constraints on the formation of infant mother: When maternal sensitivity becomes ineffective. *Infant Behavior and Development, 26,* 285-299.

Aviezer, O., van IJzendoorn, M. H., Sagi, A., & Schuengel, C. (1994). "Children of the Dream" revisited: 70 years of collective child care in Israeli kibbutzim. *Psychological Bulletin, 116,* 99-116.

Baron, R. M., & Kenny, D. A. (1986). The moderator-mediator variable distinction in social psychological research: Conceptual, strategic, and statistical considerations. *Journal of Personality and Social Psychology, 51,* 1173-1182.

Belsky, J. (1999). Interactional and contextual determinants of attachment security. In J. Cassidy & P. R. Shaver (Eds.), *Handbook of attachment: Theory, research and clinical applications* (pp. 249-264).New York: Guilford Press.

Brethterton, I. (2000). Emotional availability: An attachment perspective. *Attachment & Human Development, 2,* 233-241.

Bronfenbrenner, U. (1989). Ecological systems theory. In R.Vasta (Ed.), *Annals of Child Development: Vol. 6. Six theories of child development: Revised formulations and current issues* (pp. 189-249). Greenwich, CT: JAI Press.

De Wolff, M. S., & van IJzendoorn, M. H. (1997). Sensitivity and attachment: A meta-analysis on parental antecedents of infant attachment. *Child Development, 68,* 571-591.

Easterbrooks, M. A., & Biringen, Z. (2000). Guest editors' introduction to the special issue: Mapping the terrain of emotional availability and attachment. *Attachment & Human Development, 2,* 123-129.

Howes, C. (1999). Attachment relationships in the context of multiple caregivers. In J. Cassidy & P. R. Shaver (Eds.), *Handbook of attachment: Theory, research and clinical applications* (pp. 671-687). New York: Guilford Press.

Koren-Karie, N., Sagi-Schwartz, A., & Egoz-Mizrachi, N. (2005). Centers in Israel: The Haifa study of early childcare. *Infant Mental Health Journal, 26,* 110-126.

National Institute of Child Health and Human Development (NICHD) Early Child Care Research Network. (1997). The effects of infant child care on infant-mother attachment security. Results of the NICHD study of early child care. *Child Development, 68,* 860-879.

NICHD Early Child Care Research Network. (1996). Characteristics of infant child care: Factors contributing to positive caregiving. *Early Childhood Research Quarterly, 11,* 269–306.

NICHD Early Child Care Research Network. (1999). Child outcomes when child care center classes meet recommended standards for quality. *American Journal of Public Health, 89,* 1072–1077.

NICHD Early Child Care Research Network. (2000). Characteristics and quality of child care for toddlers and preschoolers. *Applied Developmental Science, 4,* 116–135.

Roer-Strier, D., & Rosenthal, M. K. (2001). Socialization in changing social contexts: A search for images of the "adaptive adult." *Social Work, 46,* 215-228.

Rutter, M., & O'Connor, T. G. (1999). Implications of attachment theory for child care policies. In J. Cassidy & P. R. Shaver (Eds.), *Handbook of attachment:Theory, research and clinical applications* (pp. 823-844). New York: Guilford Press.

Seginer, R. (2006). Parents' educational involvement: A developmental ecology perspective. *Parenting: Science and Practice, 6,* 1-48.

van IJzendoorn, M. H., Tavecchio, L. W. C., Stams, G-J., Verhoeven, M., & Reiling, E. (1998). Attunement between parents and professional caregivers: A comparison of childrearing attitudes in different child-care settings. *Journal of Marriage and the Family, 60,* 771-781.

Ward, M. J., & Carlson, E. A. (1995). Associations among adult attachment representations, maternal sensitivity, and infant-mother attachment in a sample of adolescent mothers. *Child Development, 66,* 69-79.

Is Maternal Behavior in the Strange Situation Related to Infant Attachment?

Janice H. Kennedy
Georgia Southern University

The relationship between infant attachment and maternal sensitivity in the Strange Situation was examined. Seventy-two mothers and their infants were videotaped in the Strange Situation. Infants were assigned to categories of secure, insecure-avoidant, anxious-resistant, or disorganized/disoriented. They were also rated on proximity-seeking, avoidance, contact-maintenance, search behavior, resistance, and distance interaction. Mothers were rated on a 9-point sensitivity scale (Ainsworth, Blehar, Waters, & Wall, 1978). Maternal sensitivity was highest for mothers of secure infants, followed by sensitivity for mothers of insecure-resistant infants. Mothers of avoidant and disoriented-disorganized infants were lowest in maternal sensitivity. Maternal sensitivity positively predicted distance interaction and was negatively related to avoidance and resistance in the Strange Situation. Consideration of maternal behavior in the Strange Situation may be a useful measure, particularly in situations where prior observation of the mother-infant relationship may not be possible. Measures of maternal sensitivity may also be more valid in the mildly stressful Strange Situation than in more familiar environments, such as the home.

In Ainsworth, Blehar, Waters, and Wall's (1978) seminal examination of maternal factors that shape the development of the caregiver-infant attachment relationship in a sample of low-risk mothers in the infant's first year, several maternal behaviors were found to predict attachment relationship quality, most notably maternal sensitivity, responsiveness, and appropriately stimulating play. Maternal sensitivity includes perceiving that a signal has occurred, interpreting it accurately, responding promptly, and responding appropriately (Ainsworth, Bell, & Stayton, 1974). Maternal sensitivity to infant signals appears to be the most salient factor related to quality of mother-infant attachment (De Wolff & van IJzendoorn, 1997),

All correspondence should be addressed to Dr. Janice H. Kennedy, Department of Psychology, Georgia Southern University, P.O. Box 8041, Statesboro, GA 30460. Electronic mail may be sent to jkennedy@georgiasouthern.edu.

and low maternal sensitivity has been reported in numerous studies of high-risk families. Maternal insensitivity has been related to depression (National Institute of Child Health and Human Development [NICHD] Early Child Care Research Network, 1999), high incidence of abuse or neglect (Carlson, Cicchetti, Barnett, & Braunwald, 1989; Lyons-Ruth, Repacholi, McLeod, & Silva, 1992), frightening or frightened behavior of the parent (Hesse & Main, 2006), inconsistent care (Bosquet & Egeland, 2001), and a subjective feeling of helplessness in mothers (Spangler & Grossman, 1999).

Children whose mothers have shown low sensitivity in parent-child interactions demonstrate poor compliance to maternal requests as toddlers (Ainsworth et al., 1974), elevated instances of psychopathology at four years (Bohlin & Hagerskull, 2000), and low school readiness and verbal comprehension in preschool (Hoffman, Crnic, & Baker, 2006). Although recent studies of maternal sensitivity (e.g., Cowan, 1997; De Wolff & van IJzendoorn, 1997; Juffer, van IJzendoorn, & Bakermans-Kranenburg, 1997; van den Boom, 1997) have generally reported less predictability for maternal sensitivity than Ainsworth originally posited for her Baltimore sample, the construct remains the most important predictor of attachment quality within the family (De Wolff & van IJzendoorn; Koren-Karie, Oppenheim, Doley, Sher, & Etzion-Carasso, 2002).

Some researchers (e.g., Thompson, 1997) have pondered why sensitive responsiveness contributes to secure attachment and how maternal sensitivity predicts later working models of self and relationships. Promptness, consistency, and appropriateness of maternal response are generally the main constituents that are used to define sensitivity (van den Boom, 1997). However, maternal sensitivity is more than a stable, maternal trait. Sroufe and Sampson (2000) point out that Ainsworth's sensitivity measures were not just the frequency of discrete maternal behaviors, but rather the interplay of behavioral patterning, surrounding context, and meaning that are necessary to understand sensitivity. They point out that sensitivity must be observed at the level of the relationship. Of course, maternal behavior is not independent of infant behavior. It is easier to be sensitive to a secure infant who gives clear signals for proximity and comfort than to an avoidant infant (who may provide few signals), or to a resistant infant (who may reject mother's offers of comfort). However, sensitivity to a particular infant's signals is a multidimensional construct that incorporates the mother's detection and interpretation of her child's signals, as well as the appropriateness and timing of her response. Ainsworth et al. (1974) believed that a mother's ability to see things from the child's point of view was necessary for serving as a secure base for exploration and the development of secure attachment. This seems to reflect the early, developing maternal side of the goal-corrected partnership that Bowlby (1969/1982) describes as unfolding in the infant's second year.

A number of studies following Ainsworth and her colleagues (1978) have examined maternal sensitivity at home (e.g., Lohaus, Keller, Ball, Voelker, & Elben, 2004), in a lab setting while the mother is playing with her infant (e.g.,

Jacobvitz, Leon, & Hazen, 2006; Smith & Pederson, 1988), or both (e.g., Bohlin & Hagekull, 2000). These studies have typically used Ainsworth's sensitivity scale or an adaptation of the instrument. While these studies have contributed to our understanding of the important correlates of security of attachment, studying sensitivity in home or free-play settings may not provide us with the level of external validity for the construct that we desire. Thompson (1997) suggests that sensitivity exhibited under nonstressful conditions may not be as predictive of typical maternal behavior as that observed under more stressful conditions.

Hundreds of studies utilizing the Strange Situation have been conducted since Ainsworth developed the procedure. Reliability across time and observers for infant classification has been good, as well as predictive and construct validity for mother-infant attachment. Attachment is viewed as a function of the mother-infant relationship (and not a characteristic of the infant alone). However, in the Strange Situation, the foci of observation are use of the mother by the infant as a secure base for exploration, infant preference for the mother over the stranger, and infant behavior in the two reunion episodes. The mother's behavior is largely restricted by the instructions to the mother to be responsive to the infant, but not to direct the infant's activities or interactions (Grossman & Grossman, 2000). However, in spite of instructions to the mother to remain in the background, there are still opportunities for considerable individual differences in how mothers react in the Strange Situation—how much they respond to infant vocalizations, how active they are in directing the infant's play, and how responsive they are in reunion episodes.

The purpose of the present study was to determine whether mother's sensitivity to the infant's needs and concerns in the Strange Situation could predict independent attachment classifications and infant attachment behaviors in mother-infant pairs. It was expected that mothers rated high in sensitivity would be more likely to have infants independently judged as secure in attachment in the Strange Situation and who would show high distance interaction and low resistance and avoidance behaviors. It was also expected that mothers rated lower in maternal sensitivity would have infants classified as disorganized/disoriented or avoidant in attachment, and their infants would show lower levels of proximity seeking, distance interaction, and contact maintenance and higher levels of resistance and/or avoidance. It was less clear as to what to expect in the relationship between maternal sensitivity and infants classified as resistant.

Method

Participants

Mothers and infants were recruited from introductory psychology, family life, and education classes in a mid-sized university, as well as from the surrounding rural community as part of a larger research project. Seventy-two mothers (M age = 28.22 years, SD = 9.50) and their infants (girls: n = 43; boys: n = 29; M age =

14.91 months, SD = 3.59) participated in the study. Seventy-seven percent were Caucasian and 23% were African-American. Forty-two percent of the infants had siblings (1-3 siblings; 5% had a younger sibling); 58% were only children. Eighty-four percent of the mothers had at least some college experience, and all but one had finished high school. Sixty (84%) of the mothers were either employed at least part-time or were college students. The child's father resided in the home in 77% (n = 55) of the cases.

Measures

Ainsworth Strange Situation and behavior ratings. This standardized procedure is a series of eight 3-minute episodes in which mother and infant are present in a playroom. It was designed by Ainsworth and her colleagues (1978) as a naturalistic observation of mother-infant attachment and exploratory behavior in a series of eight episodes increasingly stressful to the infant. Infants are exposed to a friendly adult female stranger, two brief separations from the mother, and a short period alone (see Ainsworth et al. [1978] for a full description of the procedure and coding guidelines).

The following three measures were obtained from the videotaped Strange Situation measure:

1. Mother-infant relationships were categorized into the standard organized attachment categories of secure, insecure-avoidant, and anxious-resistant and the disorganized/disoriented category (see Ainsworth et al., 1978; Main & Solomon, 1990). Assignments were based on reunion behaviors after separations from the mother (e.g., distal interaction, proximity-seeking, avoidance, resistance), using the mother as a secure base for exploration, and preference for the mother over the stranger for the organized categories (secure, avoidant, and resistant) and the presence of disoriented/disorganized behaviors for the disorganized category (see Main, Hesse, & Kaplan, 2005). Generally, infants were classified as secure if they showed friendly greeting and/or proximity seeking to the mother during reunion episodes, a strong preference for the mother over the stranger in seeking comfort when distressed, and exploration from a secure base when the mother was present. Infants were classified as avoidant if they ignored the mother during reunion episodes, their behavior to the stranger was as friendly to the stranger as to the mother, and they did not show a higher quality of play when mother was present than when she was absent. Infants were classified as resistant if they demonstrated significant anger towards the mother in reunion episodes while seeking contact with her, were clingy and unable to use the mother as a secure base for exploration, and strongly preferred the mother to the stranger. Following Main and Solomon (1990), all infants were rated on a 9-point scale for disorganized/disoriented behavior (showing atypical behaviors such as freezing or stereotypical behaviors such as hand wringing); those rated 6 or above were given a disorganized/disoriented classification as their primary category.

All 72 videotapes were coded for attachment classification by one coder trained in the Strange Situation procedure who was blind to other information about the mother and child using the standard attachment classifications of secure, insecure-avoidant, anxious-resistant, and disorganized. Thirty percent ($n = 22$) of the videotapes were randomly selected to be coded by a second trained observer for reliability purposes. When coders disagreed, a classification was assigned by consensus. Average agreement with the 4-category classification system was .88 (κ = .72).

2. Interactive behaviors of proximity-seeking, contact-maintenance, resistance, avoidance, search, and distance interaction were rated from the videotapes on a 7-point Likert-type scale (Ainsworth et al., 1978) by four trained observers who had not coded the infant and mother for attachment classification. Pearson r's for interobserver agreement ranged .66 - .88; average agreement across all behaviors and observers was Pearson $r = .79$.

3. Maternal Sensitivity was rated on a 9-point Likert-type scale (Ainsworth et al., 1974). Videotapes were scanned for infant bids for attention from the mother. Mothers' awareness of the signals, accuracy of interpretation, appropriateness of response, and promptness of response comprised the basis of global ratings of sensitivity. One researcher coded all of the videotapes, while a second researcher coded a subset of 25 randomly selected videotapes. Both coders were graduate students trained by the author of the study. Both coders were blind to attachment classification and attachment behaviors as coded above or to demographic information about the mothers and infants. Interobserver agreement for the 25 videotapes seen by both observers was Pearson $r(24) = .85$, $p < .001$.

Procedure

Mothers and infants were videotaped through a one-way mirror in an experimental playroom modeled after Ainsworth's Strange Situation room (Ainsworth et al., 1978). There were chairs for the mother and the stranger, and a child's chair surrounded by toys about 8 feet away from the adult chairs. A female graduate student experienced with young children served as the stranger. After the Strange Situation procedure, mothers completed questionnaires relevant to the larger study, along with demographic information.

Results

Attachment Classifications and Attachment Behavior Ratings

Forty-five securely attached infants, 10 insecure-avoidant infants, 9 insecure-resistant infants, and 8 disorganized infants were identified in the Strange Situation. To determine whether infant attachment classifications were related to infant behavior ratings, One-Way Analyses of Variance were conducted for proximity seeking, contact maintenance, resistance, avoidance, search, and distance interaction by attachment classification (see Table 1). All analyses were significant, except for search. Post-hoc analyses showed that anxious-resistant and disorganized infants showed highest proximity seeking and contact maintenance, followed by secure infants; avoidant infants showed the lowest levels of proximity seeking and contact maintenance. With regard to resistance, secure and avoidant infants showed the least resistance, while avoidant, resistant, and disorganized infants did not differ from one another. With regard to avoidance, avoidant infants showed high avoidance compared to infants in other categories. With regard to distance interaction, secure and resistant infants maintained higher levels of interaction than did avoidant and disorganized infants. (See Table 1 for means and standard deviations.)

Table 1

Means and Standard Deviations for Infant Attachment Behaviors by Attachment Classification

	Infant Classification					
Attachment Behavior	Secure	Avoidant	Resistant	Disorganized	F	p
	M SD	M SD	M SD	M SD		
Proximity-seeking	3.75_a (1.60)	1.86_b (.69)	6.20_c (.84)	5.86_c (1.86)	12.14	.001
Contact-maintenance	3.27_a (1.66)	1.29_b (.76)	5.80_c (1.79)	5.71_c (2.21)	11.50	.0001
Resistance	1.55_a (1.25)	2.29_{ab} (1.89)	3.80_b (2.59)	4.29_b (2.21)	7.18	.0001
Avoidance	1.97_a (1.29)	5.71_b (1.25)	2.80_a (1.30)	3.29_a (2.75)	11.67	.0001
Search	4.00_a (1.98)	3.86_a (1.95)	5.40_a (1.34)	5.57_a (1.99)	1.93	.138
Distance Interaction	3.84_a (1.62)	2.14_b (.69)	4.00_a (2.34)	2.14_b (1.07)	4.22	.01

Note. Means sharing a common subscript do not differ significantly from one another; $df = (3, 67)$

Attachment Classifications and Maternal Sensitivity

The overall mean maternal sensitivity rating was 5.19 ($SD = 1.94$). To determine whether Maternal Sensitivity ratings in the Strange Situation were associated with infant attachment classification, a One-Way Analysis of Variance was conducted, $F(3, 68) = 21.34, p = .001, \eta^2 = .47$. Post-hoc analyses showed that mothers of secure infants had the highest ratings on sensitivity ($M = 6.18, SD = 1.51$), followed by mothers of anxious-resistant infants ($M = 4.56, SD = 1.13$), and last by disorganized ($M = 3.13, SD = 1.55$) and insecure-avoidant ($M = 3.00, SD = 1.05$) infants. Ratings of disorganized/disoriented behavior were related to maternal sensitivity as well, Pearson $r(70) = -.48, p < .001$.

Attachment Behavior Ratings and Maternal Sensitivity

Relationships between maternal sensitivity ratings and behavioral ratings of distance interaction, search behavior, avoidance, resistance, and proximity seeking were computed. Maternal sensitivity was positively related to distance-interaction, Pearson $r(70) = .41$, $p = .002$, negatively related to avoidance of the mother, Pearson $r(70) = -.48$, $p = .001$, and to resistance, Pearson $r(70) = -.43$, $p = .002$. Infants of mothers rated high in sensitivity were more likely to maintain interaction across a distance and less likely to show avoidance and resistance in the Strange Situation. Maternal sensitivity was not related to infant search behavior, proximity-seeking, or contact maintenance.

With regard to demographic variables, it was noted that when fathers were absent from the home, infants were rated higher in avoidance of and resistance to their mothers, $F(1,36) = 5.39$, $p = .026$ ($Ms = 3.87$ vs. 2.36), and $F(1,36) = 3.76$, $p = .045$ ($Ms = 3.28$ vs. 2.00, respectively), although father absence was unrelated to maternal sensitivity, $t(70) = .03$, $p > .05$.

Discussion

In summary, mothers of secure infants were rated highest in sensitivity, followed by mothers of anxious-resistant infants, while mothers of avoidant and disorganized infants received the lowest ratings. Maternal sensitivity predicted high distance interaction ratings and low avoidance and resistance ratings. The impact of the father's presence in the home was unanticipated: When fathers were not present, infants were rated higher in avoidance and in resistance to their mothers in the Strange Situation.

Ainsworth's home observations (e.g., Ainsworth et al., 1974) paved the way in showing that infants' behaviors during the Strange Situation are not merely a reflection of current maternal behavior, but rather a reflection of their working models of the physical and emotional availability of the mother at moments of stress developed over the first year at home. Mothers' sensitivity as shown in the Strange Situation is associated with measures of infant attachment security as well. Rating maternal sensitivity in this setting does appear to be a useful measure, especially when earlier measures of sensitivity are not available. Vereijken, Riksen-Walraven, and Kondo-Ikemura (1997) found in their longitudinal study of Japanese mothers and their infants that maternal sensitivity was actually more stable over time in a variety of settings than infant attachment classification. Maternal sensitivity measures in the Strange Situation may in fact be more valid, given that this is a more stressful setting than when maternal sensitivity is measured in the home.

The lack of a relationship between father absence and maternal sensitivity was somewhat surprising. We know that spousal and social support (Cowan, 1997; Owen & Cox, 1997) are distal factors that support good parenting by the primary caregiver, and that stress tends to reduce maternal sensitivity (Goodman & Gotlib, 1999). Father absence may have been compensated for by other family members; single mothers reported in nearly 50% of the cases that their infants were cared for by a family member while they worked or went to school.

The current study examined infants' bids for attention from the mother, both direct (e.g., offering a toy) or indirect (e.g., standing nearby, watching the mother, holding a toy the infant does not know how to operate). Mothers' responses (yes or no) and appropriateness of the response were examined. It may be helpful in future studies to examine what mothers say to infants in this "structured" situation. Mothers sometimes said insensitive things (e.g., when the stranger exited in one episode, the mother said, "Oh, you must have hurt her feelings. She's leaving."). Other studies have reported elevated rates of disrupted affective communication (Lyons-Ruth et al., 1991) or unusual linguistic responses (Hesse & Main, 2006) with disoriented/ disorganized infants. Radke-Yarrow (1991) reported that depressed mothers focused on their own feelings rather than the feelings of their infants. Professional practitioners may wish to pay particular attention to these issues in informal observations and interviews with high-risk mothers and their infants. A relationship between parental state of mind with respect to attachment and caregiving sensitivity and attunement has been demonstrated (Bakermans-Kranenburg, van IJzendoorn, & Juffer, 2003). Moreover, considering the importance of coherence in relating one's state of mind with regard to attachment (Hesse & Main, 2006) in the Adult Attachment Interview, perhaps it is time to consider maternal behavior and speech in the Strange Situation as well.

References

Ainsworth, M. D. S., Blehar, M. C., Waters, E. C., & Wall, S. N. (1978). *Patterns of attachment: A psychological study of the strange situation.* Hillsdale, NJ: Lawrence Erlbaum Associates.

Ainsworth, M. D. S., Bell, S. M., & Stayton, D. J. (1974). Infant-mother attachment and social development: 'Socialization' as a product of reciprocal responsiveness to signals. In M. P. M. Richards (Ed.), *The integration of a child into a social world* (pp. 99-136). London: Cambridge University Press.

Bakermans-Kranenburg, M. J., van IJzendoorn, M. H., & Juffer, F. (2003). Less is more: Meta-analyses of sensitivity and attachment interventions in early childhood. *Psychological Bulletin, 129,* 195-215.

Bohlin, G., & Hagekull, B. (2000). Behavior problems in Swedish four-year-olds. In P. M. Crittenden & A. H. Claussen (Eds.), *The organization of attachment relationships: Maturation, culture, and context* (pp. 75-96). London: Cambridge University Press.

Bosquet, M., & Egeland, B. (2001). Associations among maternal depressive symptomatology, state of mind and parent and child behaviors: Implications for attachment-based interventions. *Attachment & Human Development, 3*, 173-199.

Bowlby, J. (1969/1982). *Attachment and Loss. Vol. I.. Attachment*. London: Basic Books.

Carlson, V., Cicchetti, D., Barnett, D., & Braunwald, K. (1989). Disorganized/ disoriented attachment relationships in maltreated infants. *Developmental Psychology, 25*, 525-531.

Cowan, P. A. (1997). Beyond meta-analysis: A plea for a family systems view of attachment. *Child Development, 68*, 601-603.

De Wolff, M. S., & van IJzendoorn, M. H. (1997). Sensitivity and attachment: A meta-analysis on parental antecedents of infant attachment. *Child Development, 68*, 571-591.

Goodman, S. H., & Gotlib, I. H. (1999). Risk for psychopathology in the children of depressed mothers: A developmental model for understanding mechanisms of transmissions. *Psychological Review, 106*, 458-490.

Grossman, K., & Grossman, K. E. (2000). Parents and toddlers at play. In P. M. Crittenden & A. H. Claussen (Eds.), *The organization of attachment relationships: Maturation, culture, and context* (pp. 13-37). London: Cambridge University Press.

Hesse, E., & Main, M. (2006). Frightened, threatening, and dissociative parental behavior in low-risk samples: Description, discussion, and interpretations. *Development and Psychopathology, 18*, 309-343.

Hoffman, C., Crnic, K. A., & Baker, J. K. (2006). Maternal depression and parenting: Implications for children's emergent emotion regulation and behavioral functioning. *Parenting: Science and Practice, 6*, 271-295.

Jacobvitz, D., Leon, K., & Hazan, N. (2006). Does expectant mothers' unresolved trauma predict frightened/frightening maternal behavior? Risk and protective factors. *Development and Psychopathology, 18*, 363-379.

Juffer, F., van IJzendoorn, M. H., & Bakermans-Kranenburg, M. J. (1997). Intervention in transmission of insecure attachment: A case study. *Psychological Reports, 80*, 531-543.

Koren-Karie, N., Oppenheim, D., Doley, S., Sher, E., & Etzion-Carasso, A. (2002). Mothers' insightfulness regarding their infants' internal experience: Relations with maternal sensitivity and infant attachment. *Developmental Psychology, 38*, 534-572.

Lohaus, A., Keller, H., Ball, J., Voelker, S., & Elben, C. (2004). Maternal sensitivity in interactions with three- and 12-month-old infants: Stability, structural composition, and developmental consequences. *Infant and Child Development, 13*, 235-252.

Lyons-Ruth, K., Repacholi, B., McLeod, S., & Silva, E. (1991). Disorganized attachment behavior in infancy: Short-term stability, maternal and infant correlates, and risk-related subtypes. *Development and Psychopathology, 3*, 377-396.

Main, M., Hesse, E., & Kaplan, N. (2005). Predictability of attachment behavior and representational processes at 1, 6, and 19 years of age. In K. E. Grossman, K. Grossman, & E. Waters (Eds.), *Attachment from infancy to adulthood: The major longitudinal studies* (pp. 245-304). New York: Guilford.

Main, M., & Solomon, J. (1990). Procedures for identifying infants as disorganized/disoriented during the Ainsworth Strange Situation. In M. T. Greenberg, D. Cicchetti, & E. M. Cummings (Eds.), *Attachment in the preschool years: Theory, research, and intervention* (pp. 121-160). Chicago: University of Chicago Press.

National Institute of Child Health and Human Development (NICHD) Early Child Care Research Network. (1999). Chronicity of maternal depressive symptoms, maternal sensitivity, and child functioning at 36 months. *Developmental Psychology, 35,* 1297-1310.

Owen, M. T., & Cox, M. J. (1997). Marital conflict and the development of infant-parent attachment relationships. *Journal of Family Psychology, 11,* 152-164.

Radke-Yarrow, M. (1991). Attachment patterns in children of depressed mothers. In C. M. Parks, J. Stevenson-Hinde, & P. Marris (Eds.), *Attachment across the life cycle* (pp. 115-126). New York: Routledge.

Smith, P. B., & Pederson, D. R. (1988). Maternal sensitivity and patterns of infant-mother attachment. *Child Development, 59,* 1097-1101.

Spangler, G., & Grossmann, K. (1999). Individual and physiological correlates of attachment disorganization in infancy. In J. Solomon & C. George (Eds.), *Attachment disorganization* (pp. 95-124). New York: Guilford.

Sroufe, L. A., & Sampson, M. C. (2000). Attachment theory and systems concepts. *Human Development, 43,* 321-326.

Thompson, R. A. (1997). Sensitivity and security: New questions to ponder. *Child Development, 68,* 595-597.

van den Boom, D. C. (1997). Sensitivity and attachment: Next steps for developmentalists. *Child Development, 68,* 592-597.

Vereijken, C. M. J. L., Riksen-Walraven, M., & Kondo-Ikemura, K. (1997). Maternal sensitivity and infant attachment security in Japan: A longitudinal study. *International Journal of Behavioral Development, 21,* 35-49.

Author Note

The author would like to thank Shauna Wilson, Heather Lindsay, Valerie Campbell, and Maritza Ortiz for their assistance in transcribing the videotapes, as well as the mothers and infants who donated their valuable time to participate in the study.

Positive Behavior Supports and Pediatric Feeding Disorders of Early Childhood: A Case Study

Heather Curtiss, Kathleen Armstrong, & Carol Lilly
University of South Florida College of Medicine

This article describes the Positive Behavior Support (PBS) approach utilized to help a family with a toddler diagnosed with infant and early childhood feeding disorder. Case study methodology was utilized to document this approach, which identified and addressed feeding problems of a child within the natural contexts and everyday routines provided by her family. This approach was helpful in addressing the complex issues surrounding early childhood feeding disorder. The functional assessment process was successfully utilized to derive and monitor an individualized treatment plan, implemented by caregivers within the natural context and routines of the family. Teaching and coaching caregivers to implement specific techniques and strategies to improve eating and monitor progress is critical to the success of this approach. Addressing infant and early childhood feeding disorders is a formidable task. This study describes the utilization of behavioral technology by an interdisciplinary team to understand and intervene in the natural environment with a toddler diagnosed with early childhood feeding disorder. This collaborative approach resulted in increased consumption and reduced refusals, eliminated the need for G-tube feedings, and stabilized growth.

Feeding Problems

Feeding problems are very commonly reported by families of young children, with estimates ranging from 25% of infants and young children to as high as 62% for toddlers, most of which resolve without intervention (Chatoor, 2002; Reau, Senturia, Lebailly, & Christoffel, 1996). However, if unresolved, feeding problems may result in under-nutrition, and consequently may be described as failure to thrive (Kessler & Dawson, 1999). Challenges associated with feeding include, but are not limited to: eating too little, limited food preferences or "picky eating," delays in self-feeding, difficulty in transitioning from liquids to a solid diet, inappropriate

All correspondence should be addressed to Heather Curtiss, Division of Child Development, Department of Pediatrics, 13101 N Bruce B. Downs Blvd., University of South Florida, Tampa, FL 33612. Electronic mail may be sent to hcurtiss@health.usf.edu.

mealtime behaviors, and refusal to eat.

While feeding problems are fairly common among the pediatric population, these incidences are even greater among children with disabilities, with up to 88% of parents of children with special needs reporting feeding problems (O'Brien, Repp, Williams, & Christophersen, 1991; Simbert, Minor, & McCoy, 1997). Poor nutrition can result in permanent damage and stunted mental development, as well as trigger feeding-related stress in families (Frank & Drotar, 1994; Sanders, Patel, LeGrice, & Shephard, 1993).

Multiple factors involving biological, psychosocial, and cultural influences are thought to contribute to pediatric feeding difficulties. Thus, engaging parents and caregivers in the diagnostic and therapeutic process is critical, because only they can provide accurate and comprehensive information about their child's experience (Frank & Drotar, 1994). Assessment and intervention that is family-focused and provided through a multidisciplinary team has been found to produce improved outcomes over traditional primary care management (Bithoney et al., 1991). Intervention approaches that have documented improved feeding behaviors include dyadic psychotherapy, home visiting, and behavior therapy (Kessler & Dawson, 1999). The behavior therapy interventions most commonly cited in the literature include (a) differential reinforcement (Cooper et al., 1999; Stark et al., 1993; Stark et al., 1996), (b) physical guidance of appropriate feeding response (Kerwin, 1999; Kerwin, Ahearn, Eicher, & Burd, 1995), and (c) extinction (Ahearn, Kerwin, Eicher, Shantz, & Swearingin, 1996; Cooper et al., 1999; Kerwin et al., 1995; Stark et al., 1996). Additionally, other approaches have been documented in the literature, although they are not as well evidenced, such as peer-mediated procedures to induce swallowing and food acceptance in young children, as well as backward chaining and fading procedures to treat total liquid refusal (Greer, Dorow, Williams, McCorkle, & Asnes, 1991; Hagopian, Farrell, & Amari, 1996). Of these interventions, differential attention has been demonstrated to be an effective treatment component for children of diverse ages, across diverse settings, and change agents. Whereas this treatment is effective for most feeding problems, some children with very severe feeding problems do not always respond and may require more intensive and aversive procedures such as physical guidance, extinction (non-removal of spoon), and swallow induction training (forward or backward chaining).

Positive Behavior Support Framework

This article presents a case study of a child diagnosed with Infant and Early Childhood Feeding Disorder and the implementation of Positive Behavior Support (PBS). PBS is an individualized and family-centered approach to resolving problem behavior that is applied within the natural environment and is focused on developing new skills (Fox, Dunlap, & Powell, 2002). PBS is described as both values-based and evidence-based, in that it recognizes the significance of the family system, the importance of positive interventions that are responsive to family needs and desires, and is supported by extensive behavioral research (Carr et al., 1999). In the PBS framework, the functional assessment process is utilized to develop an understanding of the purpose or function of a child's behavior from which the caregiving team and parents design an intervention plan (Carr et al., 2002; Fox, Dunlap, & Powell, 2002; Strain & Hemmeter, 1997). PBS differs from applied behavior analysis, in that (a) the intervention occurs in the natural environment (e.g., home, preschool), (b) the primary caregiver provides the intervention, while professionals serve as "coaches," and (c) the intervention provides caregivers with beneficial information to support development (Armstrong, Hornbeck, Beam, Mack, & Popkave, 2006; Joseph & Strain, 2003.)

Case Study

Background Information

Maria was delivered via C-section due to detection of an irregular heartbeat following a 30-weeks pregnancy to a 27-year-old, healthy mother. Maria weighed 2010 grams at birth. After delivery, she had difficulty breathing on her own, her heart rhythm was irregular, and consequently, she was suctioned, intubated, bagged and transferred to the Neonatal Intensive Care Unit (NICU) where she was placed on an oscillator. Over the next several days, multiple medical procedures and tests followed, including blood and chromosome analyses. During this time, Maria was diagnosed with gastroesophageal reflux (GER) and was fed through a nasogastric tube (NG tube) due to total refusal to suck and swallow. Consequently, she was also pronounced failure to thrive due to poor weight gain. After 84 days in the NICU, Maria was discharged from the hospital, sent home on an apnea monitor, and received 16 hours of daily nursing care to help parents manage the complex medical care that she required. Two weeks after Maria was discharged, she had surgery to place a gastrostomy tube (G-tube), and began receiving bolus feedings during the day and at night along with medications to help control the reflux (Reglan® and Previcid®). Her weight-for-age increased from below the 3rd percentile to the 10th percentile within a year, and the reflux continued. A swallow study was completed, indicating normal anatomy and well-coordinated muscle activity for eating. Soon after she was discharged she was also referred to the federal program for infants and toddlers with developmental delays (Part C) and began receiving early intervention in the form of speech therapy and a developmental specialist came to the home to work with her mom on developing social-emotional interactions.

As a result of the tube feedings, Maria no longer showed interest in oral feedings, and in fact consistently refused to participate in any oral feeding. Her protesting would begin as soon as parents attempted to place her in her highchair or sit with her at a table for feedings. Maria vehemently refused most offers of solid foods or drinks by initially turning away and whining, and ultimately by crying, spitting, arching her back and vomiting if parents persisted with feeding. Her parents were quite stressed as a result of these feeding problems, and reported little confidence in their ability to assist Maria in feedings.

Maria's speech therapist recommended that Maria be referred to an in-patient hospital feeding program, but Maria's family preferred to continue in-home oral-motor feeding therapy with the speech therapist. This therapy typically consisted of wrapping a piece of watermelon in gauze and placing it in Maria's mouth while she would bite down on the gauze. Maria would swallow liquids seeping through the gauze but would spit out any pieces of watermelon that remained in her mouth once the gauze was removed. Maria would engage for a brief period (three to six bites) and then tantrum. She continued to receive most of her nourishment via G-tube feedings and her growth and nutrition were monitored by a gastrointestinal specialist.

At 17 months of age, Maria and her family were referred to Helping Our Toddlers, Developing Our Children's Skills (HOT DOCS©; Armstrong, Lilly, & Curtiss, 2006), a parent training program funded by the Children's Board of Hillsborough County and offered through the Division of Child Development at the University of South Florida. HOT DOCS© is designed to assist young children with challenging behaviors and their families through the implementation of positive behavior supports. Informed consent forms were approved by the University of South Florida IRB, and were explained to the family to allow data collection and analysis.

A collaborative team was formed, which included Maria's parents, speech therapist, pediatrician, Part C early intervention provider and the PBS coach (a doctoral level school psychology graduate student). The PBS coach met with the team, explained the PBS process, and obtained consent from the parents. A functional assessment interview (FAI) was completed with the parents, speech therapist, and early intervention provider, in order to better understand the difficulties around feeding and to develop hypotheses regarding the "function" served by the challenging behavior (O'Neill et al., 1997). The FAI and intervention process took place in Maria's home, which is a hallmark of the PBS approach to providing intervention within the natural settings and everyday routines of the individual. The PBS coach continued to meet with all team members informally (in the office or over the phone) on a bi-monthly basis during intervention. These team members consulted with the PBS coach who in turn directly worked with the family. During the PBS intervention, Maria continued to receive in-home speech therapy, which now focused on developing speech and language skills; early intervention services, which targeted social and emotional skills; monthly visits to her gastrointestinal specialist; bi-yearly visits with the developmental pediatrician and her primary care pediatrician. No other medical specialists were warranted at this time.

PBS Process

Problem Identification

Functional assessment. The functional assessment interview (FAI) consists of a structured interview of parents and providers, review of records, and direct observations of the child during difficult routines (O'Neill et al., 1997). The FAI is used to gain a better understanding of how a problem behavior is governed through antecedents and maintained through consequences, as well as to identify the function underlying the problem behavior. Maria's parents were also asked to complete a two-week feeding log to document when and where her feedings occurred, whether feedings were oral or via the G-tube, who provided feedings, the type of food offered, amount consumed, and vomiting episodes in response to feedings.

Maria was provided with six meals a day, three of which were offered at traditional mealtimes (i.e., breakfast, lunch, dinner) and an additional three snacks to boost calorie consumption. At baseline, Maria was orally consuming an average of 25-33 cc of baby food per meal and drinking an average of 10 cc of formula (three times a day at breakfast, lunch, and dinner), and was supplemented with Pediasure® through G-tube feedings about six times a day (120 cc per meal and snack or about 720 cc per day). These data were collected across 4 weeks by Maria's mother and provided to the PBS coach who analyzed them to provide a baseline for evaluation. In summary, most of Maria's calories were consumed through the use of a G-tube across meals during baseline and she averaged 40 cc of oral food and drink consumption per traditional meal. Medium chain triglycerides (MCT) oil was added to her baby food to increase caloric intake.

Review of Maria's medical records indicated that the *Developmental Assessment of Young Children* (DAYC; Voress & Maddox, 1998) had been completed at 3 months, 8 months, and again at 21 months of age and scores were adjusted for 10 weeks prematurity for eligibility for Part C services and progress monitoring (see Table 1). The DAYC assesses developmental accomplishments in the domains of cognitive, communication, social-emotional, physical, and adaptive behavior, and provides both age equivalents and standard scores. The assessment at 21 months indicated that Maria's development continued to lag behind her peers with respect to communication (age equivalent 13 months), and adaptive behavior (age equivalent 12 months; mostly due to limited feeding skills). Additionally, a standard growth chart (Ross Products, 1982) was used to document Maria's height, weight, and head circumference at baseline. Her calculated weight and height were both at the 25th percentile (weight-for-height = 25th percentile), which was utilized as a baseline measure to monitor her growth and ensure safety of this intervention.

Behavioral observations were completed in Maria's home on a bi-monthly basis, prior to and during lunch and/or snack times. Maria would start whining and squirming when placed in her highchair. When food was placed in front of her, she would turn her head, push the food away, and occasionally kick. If her mother or the speech therapist persisted and placed food in her mouth (yogurt or Stage III baby food), Maria would frequently gag herself until she vomited, which occurred at a rate of 1.45 times per day.

Table 1
Results of the Developmental Assessment of Young Children (DAYC)

	3 months		8 months		21 months	
Domain	Age score	Standard score	Age score	Standard score	Age score	Standard score
Physical	Birth	80	Birth[b]	71	20	99
Social-Emotional	3	100	4[b]	81	15	87
Adaptive	Birth	80	2[b]	75	12[b]	78
Cognitive	2	95	4[b]	80	17	75
Communication	1	93	3[b]	85	13[b]	62

Note. For pre-term infants, scores obtained on the DAYC are compared to the child's adjusted age. Age scores are for adjusted age due to premature birth.
[a] $M = 100$, $SD = 15$. [b] Denotes 25% delay in developmental domain.

Support Plan Development

The PBS team including the parents utilized the FAI to formulate a support plan, which was recorded visually on chart paper (see Table 2). The top portion of the support plan is used to identify and understand the problem behavior. Steps in this process include (a) describing the problem behavior, (b) describing the antecedents or triggers to the problem behavior, and (c) documenting the consequences that are maintaining the problem behavior. A central part of the PBS model is to create a hypothesis about the function of the problem behavior. In other words, a central goal is to teach the parents what the child obtains (e.g., attention, a toy) or escapes from (e.g., eating, taking a bath, going to bed) for engaging in the behavior, and this too was listed on the chart.

In the case of Maria, the team documented that she engaged in the following challenging behaviors at mealtimes: whining, crying, turning away, pushing food away, arching her back, gagging and vomiting. The antecedents or triggers occurred when Maria was placed in her high chair (whining) and when food was presented (pushing food away, gagging, etc.).

Table 2
Maria's Support Plan

Triggers What happens before the behavior?	Behavior	Consequences What happens after the behavior?
• Mother puts maria in highchair for feeding • Maria is presented with food	• Maria whines/cries • Maria kicks/turns head • Maria gags/vomits on food ┌─ **Function:** ─┐ │ **Get attention Escape** │ └─ **feeding** ─┘	• Caregiver provides attention • Caregiver wipes her face • Caregiver takes Maria out of highchair
Preventions	**New Skills**	**New Responses**
• Show Maria schedule of mealtimes • Institute mean and snack routine into daily schedule • Feed in highchair only • Adult eats with her model eating • Read Maria Likes to Eat and "first/then" board • Use timer to indicate begininng and end of meal	• Maria sits in her highchair • Maria drinks liquids from a cup • Maria tastes foods • Maria chews/swallows foods • Maria self-feeds with fingers • Maria says "all done" when full	• Offer enthusiastic praise and attention • Successful feeding followed with highly preferred activity • Ignore avoidance behaviors and redirect to meal ("It's time to eat.") • Validate her feelings ("I know this is hard, but you can do it.")

The response to these escalating behaviors was twofold: Maria's parents would stop feeding her and generally allow her to return to play activities. Thus, it seemed that the *function* of Maria's behavior was to avoid eating solid foods.

The team hypothesized that Maria had missed opportunities to develop pleasurable responses associated with mealtimes because of the discomfort associated with GER early feedings for which Maria was still taking medication. Although her mother believed that Maria no longer experienced the discomfort, Maria's distress around oral feeding interfered with her ability to recognize internal hunger cues, seek out her parents for this comfort, and establish regular eating patterns. Likewise, instead of responding to their baby's cues for hunger, Maria's parents had focused their attention on supporting her medical needs. They had become quite vigilant about the G-tube feedings, which had replaced the normal feeding relationship. Maria had developed neither the expected oral-motor skills associated with feeding such as chewing and swallowing food, nor the expected social and communication skills such as finger feeding and asking for food.

Intervention strategies developed by the team to solve these problems were categorized as: (a) preventions, (b) new skills, and (c) new responses, and were documented on the bottom of the support plan. Preventions refer to changes that signal and increase predictability of the routine and promote independence, thus minimizing the antecedents to the problem behavior. New skills refer to the replacement behaviors needed by the child to achieve new milestones. New responses refer to adult responses which serve to reinforce new learning, or redirect problem behavior.

Prevention strategies included establishing regular mealtimes in 3-hour intervals to regulate her body clock and to help her establish eating patterns. The pediatrician recommended discontinuation of nighttime G-tube feedings in order to promote appetite, and thus increase motivation to eat food. Parents were encouraged to enthusiastically offer food first, then liquids, and only use the G-tube when Maria did not consume a minimum of 118 cc of food or formula by mouth. Meal and snack times were to take place only when Maria was seated in her highchair, which was positioned at the family table, and parents were encouraged to eat with her. Meals and snacks were limited to 20-25 minutes, and parents began using a digital timer to signal the end of meals. All other distracters such as television and toys were eliminated during mealtimes.

To help Maria learn developmentally appropriate feeding skills, a social story was developed which depicted a child seated in a highchair happily eating. Social stories are tools that were originally developed for children with Autism to help them understand events, expectations, and more effective responses. Pictures used in the story included: Maria sitting in her high chair with a variety of solid foods and drinks on her place setting; demonstrations of tasting, chewing and swallowing; and playing happily with her mother after mealtime. Other visual supports included use of a "First-Then" board, a support based upon the Premack Principle that one will engage in less desired behavior if it is followed by desired behavior (Lentini, Vaughn, & Fox, 2005).

Maria's mother collected all the data on Maria's food consumption. She already knew how to measure Maria's food in cc and thus, the PBS coach created her paper and pencil logs as well as a Microsoft Excel spreadsheet for logging the data. Maria's mother would write down what Maria ate on the paper after each meal and then transfer this data to the Excel spreadsheet each Friday. Once a month she provided the paper logs and the electronic log to the PBS coach for data analysis. This system was convenient, and according to Maria's mother, it was easy for her to use. Each month the PBS coach shared Maria's progress with her mother by making graphs of her progress from the previous 4 weeks. Data integrity checks were conducted by the PBS coach at the end of the month whereby the paper logs were reconciled with the electronic log.

Support Plan Implementation

Support plan implementation includes both teaching and coaching components. Teaching new skills involves setting a goal, which is broken down into the component parts, modeled, and reinforced throughout the day (Ostrosky & Sandall, 1999). Maria's support plan was ultimately implemented in three phases whereby Maria's "New Skills" were gradually adjusted as she progressed with feeding skills, and as her parents became more confident in their role. Throughout the intervention, caregivers were encouraged to offer attention and praise only when Maria cooperated with feedings, and to ignore and redirect her when she engaged in challenging behaviors. The coaching component involved the PBS coach meeting with Maria and her mother on a bi-monthly basis to build a collaborative relationship with the mother, to integrate the mother's beliefs about how to feed her child into the support plan, to coach her through implementation of new skills, and to role-model the use of these skills during lunches wherein the PBS coach, Maria, and her mother ate together.

Phase I. In phase I, the goal of intervention was to increase the amount of calories consumed orally and ultimately to eliminate the use of the G-tube feedings. The steps to achieve this goal included (a) seating Maria in her highchair for all meals and snacks, (b) offering her solid food, followed by fluids in a sippy cup, (c) attending to and encouraging interest in feeding, and (d) administering G-tube feeds only during the last 5 minutes of meals. Maria's mother found that she was much more interested in drinking from a cup and straw, which was substituted for the sippy cup. Figure 1 summarizes Maria's progress after approximately 1 month of intervention.

At first, Maria responded positively, increasing the amount of calories consumed orally from approximately 40 cc per meal before intervention to 100 cc per meal and 75 cc per snack. Use of the G-tube decreased from approximately 80 cc per meal to 60 cc per meal. The pediatrician believed that Maria was consuming enough nutrition to support adequate growth which was documented as her weight-for-height which remained at the 25th percentile. Vomiting episodes had reduced from 1.45 to 0.61 times per day.

Figure 1
Average consumption of calories across traditional meals and snacks.

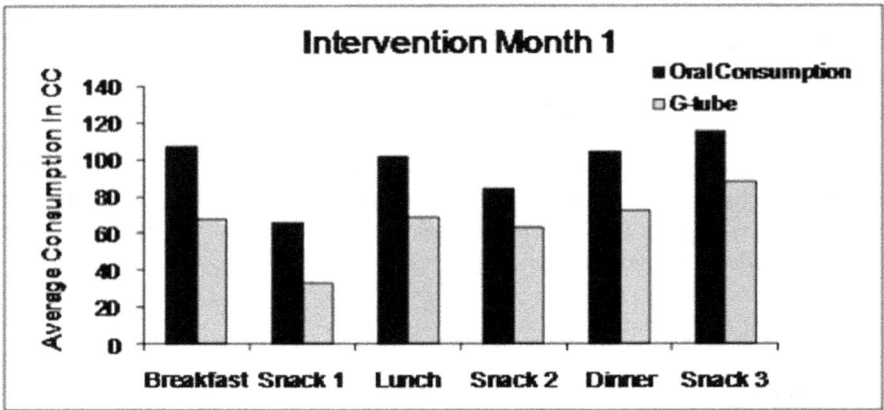

In the third month, G-tube feedings had only been used for one meal and Maria was consuming approximately 180 cc per meal and 80 cc per snack (see Figure 2). Her food choices had expanded to yogurt, milkshakes, and formula. Maria selected her choice by pointing to the item. Her average consumption over the month included: yogurt ($M = 23$ cc per snack time chosen), milkshake ($M = 34$ cc per snack time chosen), and formula ($M = 39$ cc per snack time chosen). Thus, after 12 weeks of intervention, Maria made tremendous progress in her willingness to engage in oral feedings of liquids and semi-solid foods, her vomiting decreased, and her weight was maintained.

However, at the beginning of the fourth month, Maria's vomiting episodes reoccurred at least daily, which her mother attributed to a reoccurrence of GER as a result of increased oral food intake. Maria lost 1 kg and, at the same time, grew 3.81 cm, thus her weight-for-height declined to the 3rd percentile. She continued to consume most of her calories orally from formula (about 143 cc per meal and 120 cc per snack time) and averaged about 25 cc of food during meal times, and subsequently refused anything but formula during the snack time. As such, the G-tube was utilized to supplement calorie intake at meals and snacks (about 60 and 80 cc, respectively) for approximately 2 weeks. Maria's weight increased to the 8th percentile and she increased her oral consumption to 180-200 cc per meal/snack so the supplemental G-tube feedings were suspended at this time.

Phase II. At the end of the sixth month of intervention and just before Maria's second birthday, the team decided that it was time to increase the quantity of foods Maria would accept and reduce her intake of formula. The plan included continued presentation of foods (e.g., baby foods, yogurt, pudding, cereal, or some other soft food), followed by the opportunity to sip formula. If Maria did not feed herself at least 25 cc of food, her mother agreed to spoon-feed her. Figure 3 summarizes results of the seventh month of intervention.

Figure 2.
Average consumption in cc per meal in month 3 of intervention.

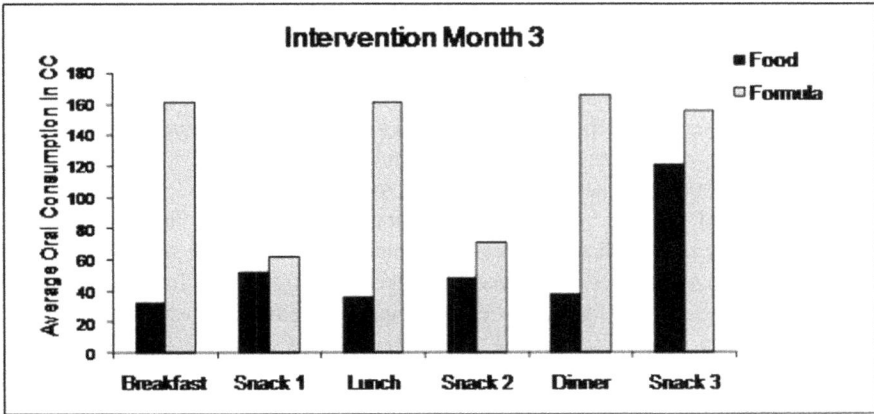

Figure 3
Average oral consumption in cc per meal in month 7 of intervention.

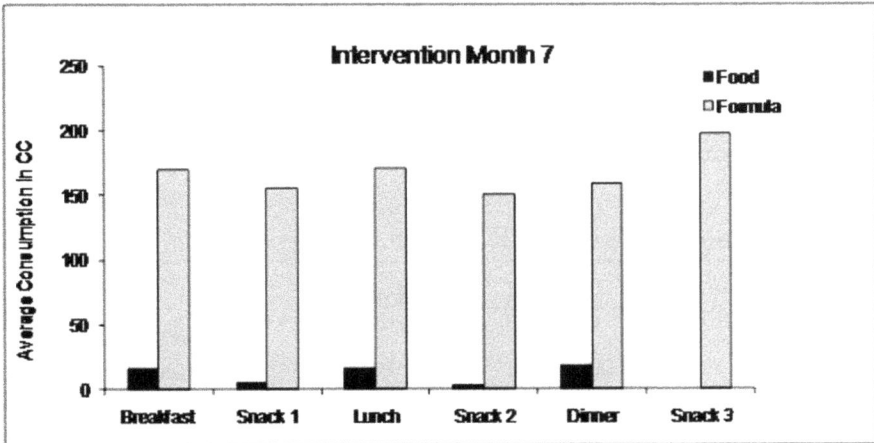

Maria responded to her mother's feeding attempts by whining, crying, arching her back, and vomiting. Vomiting episodes increased slightly to about 1.7 times per day. The G-tube was not utilized during this month. Maria's mother reported that trying to force Maria to eat was too stressful for her and that she could not continue. Thus, Maria's consumption of solid foods decreased slightly but oral liquid consumption remained stable and adequate for nutritional needs. She did agree to gently coax Maria to self-feed, but could not persist when Maria began refusing. She also offered Maria more choices of solid foods that are generally enjoyed by toddlers, such as eggs, crackers, waffles, cheese, and other finger foods.

Over the next 6 months of intervention, Maria's mother had significantly reduced her attempts to get Maria to eat solid foods, finally offering solid foods only during breakfast, lunch and dinner. Maria was eating between 0-20 cc of food at breakfast and lunch, and 30 cc of food at dinner, followed by drinking her formula. In all, Maria was consuming about 180 cc and 150 cc of formula during meals and snacks, respectively. Thus, although Maria was consuming her calories orally, she did not make significant progress toward transitioning to solid foods. Because Maria was gaining weight (weight-for-height at 10th percentile) by drinking formula and not vomiting as frequently, her gastrointestinal (GI) specialist did not encourage her mother's attempts to transition Maria to solid foods.

Phase III. In the 14th month of intervention, Maria's mother indicated readiness to cutback on formula feedings and focus on solid foods to promote Maria's continued development. She understood that Maria would likely be resistant, and that she would need to consistently present solid foods, provide an adequate opportunity to eat solid foods, and only offer formula at the end of meals. For snack time, Maria's mother agreed to only offer solid foods and eliminate the choice of formula in an effort to increase Maria's hunger and desire to eat.

As expected, Maria resisted eating solid foods and consumed very small amounts (about 21 cc) across traditional meals and would not accept anything during snack times. In addition, the amount of formula she would accept decreased to 110 cc per meal, for a combined oral intake of 120 cc across meals (Figure 4). Consequently, Maria's mother decided to administer the remaining formula (about 90 cc per meal) via G-tube. In addition, Maria's mother administered an additional 116 cc of formula, on average, through the G-tube at snack 3 to increase caloric intake. This cycle continued through the remainder of the month, and Maria's weight-for-height remained at the 10th percentile.

Figure 4
Average consumption in cc per meal in month 14 of intervention.

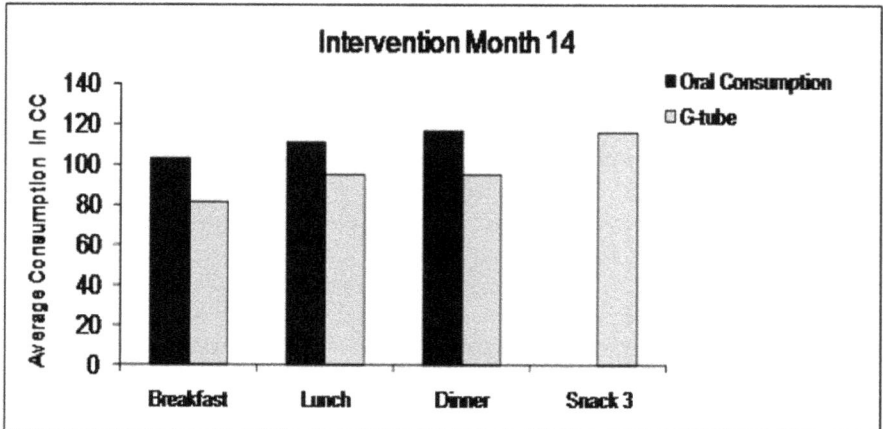

By the 15th month of intervention, Maria's mother was ready to eliminate the use of the G-tube for at least 2 weeks to see if Maria could maintain weight without the supplemental calories. Within days, Maria was consuming a significant amount of foods orally at meals and snacks (about 86 and 70 cc, respectively). Maria continued to maintain weight and actually gained 113.39 gms over two weeks without use of the G-tube and thus, weight-for-height remained stable at the 10th percentile. The formula was replaced with milk, soy milk, juice, and milkshake drinks and Maria averaged 99 cc of liquids per meal and about 85 cc of solid food. At snacks, Maria was only offered water and solid food. She ate about 70 cc of solid food per snack across the month. From this point forward, Maria continued to increase her consumption of solid foods and to decrease high-calorie liquids and as such, it became difficult for Maria's mother to quantify the amount in cc. However, Maria was gaining weight (height-for-weight at the 20th percentile) and the G-tube was no longer being utilized. Figure 5 displays data across meals and snacks for month 15 of intervention.

Figure 5
Average oral consumption in cc per meal and snack in month 15 of intervention.

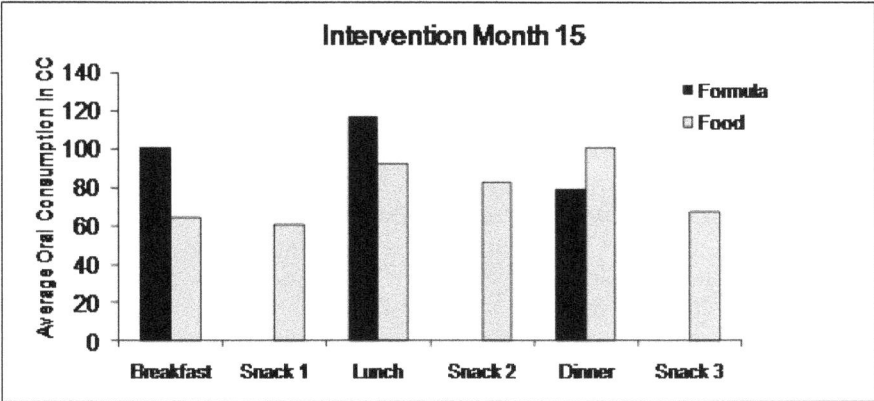

Discussion

Although Maria responded immediately to the feeding intervention as demonstrated by a reduction of tube feedings and willingness to consume liquids, it was much more challenging to help her transition to solid foods. And, although there was an initial decrease in vomiting behaviors, the episodes returned, and continued to occur, in response to feeding until the 13th month of treatment. It is difficult to determine whether vomiting was triggered by reoccurrence of GER or by intense distress associated with feedings or by a combination. Nonetheless, Maria's intense reactions and refusals with feeding contributed to the difficulty her mother had in following through with the intervention.

However, now Maria willingly eats a variety of foods, is growing adequately, and making good progress across other areas of development. Vomiting episodes have virtually disappeared, and with it, much of her parents' stress. Maria's G-tube has been removed because it is no longer beneficial to her health. Her family has established regular and enjoyable mealtimes. Maria's everyday quality of life has improved, now that the focus has been removed from the feeding issue. She is attending preschool, making friends, and participating in community activities that offer her opportunities to explore, experiment, and learn about her world.

Lessons Learned

The primary lesson learned by this study was of the complexity in addressing feeding disorders, resulting from major medical problems, reactions of distress around eating, and disruptions of both the feeding relationship and regulation of feeding patterns. This child spent the first 3 months of her life in a hospital, in a life-threatening situation.

When she finally was allowed to come home to her parents, her medical needs prevented formation of regular feeding patterns, and likely the attachment which develops along with feeding. And even as she made progress with the intervention, she continued to resist self-feedings and her mother's attempts to feed her.

Limitations

First, there were many providers involved in Maria's care, and while we attempted to engage them in the PBS process, a critical provider (the GI specialist) was not able to participate on the team. This provider expectedly had a focus on maintaining Maria's weight gain and less interest in her development of feeding skills. Thus, his influence may have been part of the family's decisions to return to G-tube feedings when Maria's refusals became too difficult for them to handle.

Second, although there were multiple providers involved in different aspects of care for Maria, the mother's mental health needs were not being addressed to the extent that she felt confident in her parenting role and ability to nourish her child. The monthly coaching visits may not have been sufficient to build a relationship with the mother or sufficient enough to off-set the severity of her child's reactions to her attempts at feeding. Additionally, Maria's father was frequently unable to assist and support Maria's mother due to a busy work schedule.

Finally, a limitation to this study certainly includes the length of time (15 months) needed to substantiate change. Over 15 months, it is expected that a child would gain many adaptive skills due to maturation. However, given the complications of this situation, it is probably safe to suggest that this child's feeding would not have improved just with time.

Conclusions

This case study is an example of the application of PBS strategies to address a toddler with a feeding disorder associated with early insult to the GI tract and consequently, who was G-tube fed. PBS is an empirically supported intervention process that has been designed to promote healthy development and improve relationships through the systematic implementation of positive supports within natural settings and everyday routines. PBS helps families and other caregivers to understand behavior, and gives them strategies to promote development by teaching children new skills. Families are critical participants throughout the PBS process, and ultimately, become their child's primary interventionist. The PBS process serves to empower families, thereby increasing their confidence and competence to address both present and future challenges that all children experience in some degree throughout their development.

Future research should continue to test the application of this approach with other children with pediatric feeding disorders. Because feeding problems are so complex, individual, and generally not attributable to a single cause, single subject methodology may offer promise for research in future applications. PBS offers promise to the field of pediatric psychology because it is a highly individualized problem-solving process, which has demonstrated effectiveness applying the science of behavior to help individuals with significant behavioral and developmental challenges. Because PBS takes place within the natural routines of the child and family, the new skills are more likely to generalize than skills learned in more traditional, clinical settings. Finally, PBS is a collaborative process that takes into account the contributions of families and professionals necessarily involved in the clinical care of these children.

References

Ahearn, W., Kerwin, M., Eicher, P., Shantz, J., & Swearingin, W. (1996). An alternating treatments comparison of two intensive interventions for food refusal. *Journal of Applied Behavior Analysis, 29,* 321-332.

Armstrong, K., Hornbeck, M., Beam, B., Mack, K., & Popkave, K. (2006). Evaluation of a curriculum designed for caregivers of young children with challenging behavior. *Journal of Early Childhood and Infant Psychology, 2,* 51-61.

Armstrong, K., Lilly, C., & Curtiss, H. (2006). *Helping our toddlers developing our children's skills.* Tampa, FL: University of South Florida, Department of Pediatrics, Division of Child Development.

American Psychiatric Association. (2000). *Diagnostic and statistical manual of mental disorders* (4th ed. TR). Washington, DC: Author.

Bithoney, W. G., McJunkin, J., Michalek, J., Snyder, J., Egan, H., & Epstein, D.

(1991). The effect of a multidisciplinary team approach on weight gain in nonorganic failure to thrive children. *Developmental and Behavioral Pediatrics, 12,* 254-258.

Carr, E. G., Dunlap, G., Horner, R., Koegel, R., Turnbull, A., & Sailor, W. (2002). Positive behavior support: Evolution of an applied science. In L. M. Bambara, G. Dunlap, & I. S. Schwartz (Eds.), *Positive behavior support: Critical articles on improving practice for individuals with severe disabilities* (pp. 45-58). PRO-ED, Inc. and TASH.

Carr, E. G., Horner, R. H., Turnbull, A. P., Marquis, J. G., McLaughlin, D., McAtee, M. L., et al. (1999). *Positive behavior support for people with developmental disabilities: A research synthesis.* Washington, DC: American Association on Mental Retardation.

Chatoor, I. (2002). Feeding disorders in infants and toddlers: Diagnosis and treatment. *Child and Adolescent Psychiatry, 11,* 163-183.

Cooper, L., Wacker, D., Brown, K., McComas, J., Peck, S., Drew, J., et al. (1999). Use of a concurrent operants paradigm to evaluate positive reinforcers during treatment of food refusal. *Behavior Modification, 23,* 3-40.

Dorow, L., Williams, G., & McCorkle, N. (1991). Peer-mediated procedures to induce swallowing and food acceptance in young children. *Journal of Applied Behavior Analysis, 24,* 783-790.

Fox, L., Dunlap, G., & Powell, D. (2002). Young children with challenging behavior: Issues and considerations for behavioral support. *Journal of Positive Behavior Interventions, 4*(4), 208-217.

Frank, D. A., & Drotar, D. (1994). Failure to thrive. In R. M. Reece (Ed.), *Child abuse: Medical diagnosis, treatment and management* (pp. 298-324). Philadelphia: Lea & Febiger.

Greer, R. D., Dorow, L., Williams, G., McCorkle, N., & Asnes, R. (1991). Peer-mediated procedures to induce swallowing and food acceptance in young children. *Journal of Applied Behavior Analysis, 24,* 783-790.

Hagopian, L., Farrell, D., & Amari, A. (1996). Treating total liquid refusal with backward chaining and fading. *Journal of Applied Behavior Analysis, 29,* 573-575.

Horner, R. H., Dunlap, G., Koegel, R. L., Carr, E. G., Sailor, W., Anderson, J., et al. (1990). Toward a technology of "nonaversive" behavioral support. *Journal of the Association of Persons with Severe Handicaps, 15,* 125-132.

Joseph, G. E., & Strain, P. S. (2003). Comprehensive evidence-based social-emotional curricula for young children: An analysis of efficacious adoption potential. *Topics in Early Childhood Special Education, 23*(2), 65-77.

Kerwin, M. (1999). Empirically supported treatments in pediatric psychology: Severe feeding problems. *Journal of Pediatric Psychology, 24,* 193-214.

Kerwin, M., Ahearn, W., Eicher, P., & Burd, D. (1995). The costs of eating: A behavioral economic analysis of food refusal. *Journal of Applied Behavior Analysis, 28*, 245-260.

Kessler, D., & Dawson, P. (Eds.). (1999). *Failure to thrive and pediatric undernutrition.* Baltimore: Paul H. Brookes Publishing Co.

Lentini, R., Vaughn, B. J., & Fox, L. (2005). *Creating teaching tools for young children with challenging behavior* [CD-ROM]. Tampa, FL: Early Intervention Positive Behavior Support, The Division of Applied Research and Educational Support.

O'Brien, S., Repp, A. C., Williams, G. E., & Christophersen, E. R. (1991). Pediatric feeding disorders. *Behavior Modification, 15*, 394-418.

O'Neill, R. E., Horner, R. H., Albin, R. W., Sprague, J. R., Storey, K., & Newton, J. S. (1997). *Functional assessment and program development for problem behavior.* Pacific Grove, CA: Brookes/Cole.

Ostrosky, M., & Sandall, S. (2001). *Teaching strategies: What to do to support young children's development.* Longmont, Co: Sopris West.

Reau, N. R., Senturia, Y. D., Lebailly, S. A., & Christoffel, K. K. (1996). Infant and toddler feeding patterns and problems: Normative data and a new direction. *Journal of Developmental & Behavioral Pediatrics, 17*, 149-153.

Ross Products. (1982). Adapted from: Hamill, P. V., Drizd, T. A., Johnson, C. L., Reed, R. B., Roche, A. F., & Moore, W. M. (1979). Physical Growth: National Center for Health Statistics percentiles. *American Journal of Clinical Nutrition, 32*, 607-629.

Sanders, M. R., Patel, R. K., Le Grice, B., & Shepherd, R. W. (1993). Children with persistent feeding difficulties: An observational analysis of the feeding interactions of problem and non-problem eaters. *Health Psychology, 12*, 64-73.

Simbert, V., Minor, J., & McCoy, J. (1997). Intensive feeding training with retarded children. *Behavioral Modification, 1*, 517-529.

Stark, L., Knapp, L., Bowen, A., Powers, S., Jelalian, E., Evans, S., et al. (1993). Increasing calorie consumption in children with cystic fibrosis: Replication with 2-year follow-up. *Journal of Applied Behavior Analysis, 26*, 435-450.

Stark, L., Mulvihill, M., Powers, S., Jelalian, E., Keating, K., Creveling, S., et al. (1996). Behavioral intervention to improve calorie intake of children with cystic fibrosis: Treatment versus wait list control. *Journal of Pediatric Gastroenterology & Nutrition, 22*, 240-253.

Strain, P. S., & Hemmeter, M. L. (1997). Keys to being successful when confronted with challenging behaviors. *Young Exceptional Children, 1*(1), 2-8.

Voress, J. K., & Maddox, T. M. (1998). *Developmental Assessment of Young Children.* Austin: Pro-Ed.

An Evaluation of the Children's Behavior Questionnaire for Use with Children from Low-Income Families

Heather Richard
Department of Psychological and Brain Sciences
University of Louisville, Louisville, KY

Deborah Winders Davis
Department of Pediatrics
University of Louisville, Louisville, KY

Barbara M. Burns
Department of Psychological and Brain Sciences
University of Louisville, Louisville, KY

Children from low-income families are at risk for developmental delays. Child factors, such as temperament, are associated with such outcomes. The Children's Behavior Questionnaire (CBQ) is widely used to measure temperament. It was validated using a large, diverse sample; however, use of the CBQ has been extended to children of poverty and no validation data are available for that population. This paper examines two studies that used two versions of the CBQ to measure temperament of children from low-income families. The studies included 100 children ages 4-5 years and 215 children ages 3-7 years, respectively. Results suggest a similar factor-loading pattern as that reported by Rothbart and colleagues with the exception of inhibitory control. Possible explanations are discussed.

All correspondence should be addressed to Dr. Deborah Winders Davis, Child Development Unit, 571 S. Floyd Street (Suite 300), Louisville, KY 40202. Electronic mail may be sent to dwdavis@louisville.edu.

The effects of poverty on children's later development have been well documented. In particular, research has demonstrated that children living in poverty are at greater risk for poor academic achievement as well as specific behavioral problems than their more affluent peers (Brooks-Gunn, Linver, & Fauth, 2005; Brooks-Gunn, Rouse, & McLanahan, 2007). Temperament is an important factor that has emerged in the literature in relation to children's academic performance and behavior (Bates, Dodge, Pettit, & Ridge, 1998; Lengua, 2002). Historically, temperament has been linked to personality and behavioral qualities of people well into adulthood (Rothbart, Ahadi, & Evans, 2000). In the early 1900s, normative research on temperament in children revealed striking individual differences. More recent longitudinal data have confirmed the high variability and stability of temperament and have led to the development of several validated measures of the constructs underlying temperament (Rothbart & Bates, 1998; Rothbart, Chew, & Gartstein, 2001). The Children's Behavior Questionnaire (CBQ) is one such measure developed by Rothbart and colleagues and is broadly used in psychological and social research. Rothbart and colleagues have demonstrated validity and reliability of the CBQ in normative samples of children (Rothbart, Ahadi, Hershey, & Fisher, 2001). The CBQ has since been used with various populations of children, including children living in poverty (Harris, Robinson, Chang, & Burns, 2007; Martini, Root, & Jenkins, 2004). This paper reviews evidence from samples of children from low-income families to determine the appropriateness of using the CBQ with this population.

Various versions of the CBQ have been reported in the literature due to the emergent nature of the instrument. An early version consisting of 204 items has been used and validated for use in a sample of children born with low birth weight from the United States (Davis, Chang, & Burns, 2006) and from Norway (Nygaard, Smith, & Torgersen, 2002). Rothbart and colleagues later dropped some items resulting in a 195-item version that is more commonly reported in the literature (Rothbart, 1996; Rothbart, Ahadi et al., 2001). These items were developed using a predominantly white, middle-class sample, but have been validated for use with other populations (Ahadi, Rothbart, & Ye, 1993; Rothbart, Ahadi et al., 2001). Specific sample characteristics in terms of race and socioeconomic indicators were not presented (Rothbart, Ahadi et al., 2001). The 195-item CBQ has not been validated for use with low-income samples. Subsequently, additional versions (short and very short forms) have been developed (Putnam & Rothbart, 2006). Putnam and Rothbart examined reliability and validity indicators of the shorter versions of the instrument in both a white, middle-income sample and a sample of racially diverse (48% African American, 34% White, and 18% Other), low-income families (49% living in poverty). More data are needed on low-income samples to determine the appropriateness of using the CBQ with low-income families.

Poverty and Child Development

There has been a considerable amount of research examining the effects of poverty on children's development in the past few decades. This has led to some important findings in the realm of academic achievement. For example, several studies have shown that children from low-income families consistently have lower scores on standardized measures of academic achievement relative to those from middle- to high-income households (Brooks-Gunn, Klebanov, & Duncan, 1996; Ramey & Campbell, 1991). In addition, children of poverty are at greater risk for poor attendance, dropping out (Cairns, Cairns, & Neckerman, 1989; Janosz, Le Blanc, Boulerice, & Tremblay, 2000), behavioral problems (Ackerman, Brown, & Izard, 2004; Lengua, 2002), and grade retention (Campbell & Ramey, 1994). These factors lead to real-life inequalities in adulthood in areas such as college admittance, job placement, and income (Kane, 1998; Orr, 2003). It is apparent from the research that early success in school is an important factor for later quality of life. Due in large part to these inequalities, researchers have explored the factors, such as temperament, that may account for the differences in developmental outcomes of children living in poverty. By understanding the developmental processes that underlie these differences, it may be possible to intervene with children who are at particular risk for adverse outcomes.

Temperament and Child Development

There is a general consensus that child development is the result of interactions between child and environmental factors. Although the specific cause-and-effect mechanisms are not clearly delineated, several factors have been associated with developmental outcomes. For example, temperament is an important child factor that has been strongly linked to behavioral and academic achievement outcomes in children. Temperament has been thought of as the basis for humans' developing personality (Rothbart, Ahadi et al., 2000) and has been broadly described as individual differences in self-regulation and reactivity (Rothbart & Derrryberry, 1981). It has been found to be highly variable across the population and relatively stable over time. Infants are thought to be biologically predisposed to particular capacities for self-regulation and reactivity; however, it has been demonstrated that these capacities can be greatly influenced by their experiences (Rothbart & Bates, 1998). This suggests that environmental factors during development interact with innate qualities of the infant in shaping temperament.

Due to the important role that temperament plays in children's developmental outcomes, many researchers have directed their efforts toward developing methods to measure temperament in young children (Rothbart, Chew, & Gartstein, 2001). Early research on temperament was based on data from the seminal work of the New York Longitudinal Study (NYLS; Thomas, Chess, Birch, Hertzig, & Korn, 1963). The

NYLS elicited several dimensions thought to be associated with temperament based on infant data, including activity level, approach/withdrawal, adaptability, mood, threshold, intensity, distractibility, rhythmicity, and attention span/persistence. However, a great deal of overlap exists between the NYLS definitions for these dimensions and it has been suggested that they do not adequately account for the developmental nature of temperament (Rothbart, Chew et al., 2001). Because of this, temperament researchers have developed new methods for assessing temperament for use throughout the course of childhood. In particular, Rothbart and colleagues have developed theoretically driven measures that are sensitive to the variable nature of temperament and its developmental progression into late childhood. One specific instrument is the CBQ for use with children ages 3 to 7 (Rothbart, 1996).

Characteristics of the Children's Behavior Questionnaire

Factor analysis of the CBQ has revealed 15 dimensions, which have been clustered into 3 factors: Effortful Control, Extraversion, and Negative Affect (Rothbart, Ahadi et al., 2001). Negative Affect is thought to involve negative emotionality, including discomfort, sadness, fear, and frustration. Extraversion involves positive emotionality, including impulsivity, activity level, and high intensity pleasure. The third factor, Effortful Control, involves self-regulatory processes, such as inhibitory and attentional control. The latter factor, in particular, has been strongly linked to developmental outcomes in the realm of academic achievement.

The validity of these three factors was evaluated using a large, diverse sample (Rothbart, 1996); however, several studies have extended the use of the CBQ specifically to children in poverty (Harris et al., 2007; Martini et al., 2004). Currently, no data are available regarding the validity of the CBQ for use in this population. Some studies of children living in poverty have found associations between effortful control as measured by the CBQ and accuracy on other attentional measures and, in particular, the ability to control behavior and inhibit voluntary responses (Chang & Burns, 2005). This is in agreement with results found in research using the CBQ in the general population. Also, similar to the general population, individual differences in effortful control have been demonstrated among children living in poverty (Li-Grining, 2007). The current paper examines two studies that used two versions of the CBQ (195-items and 98-items) to measure temperament in samples of children from low-income families. The first study included 100 children ages 4-5 years from Head Start programs. The second included 215 children from 3-7 years of age recruited from local Head Start programs or a medical clinic that serves children from low-income families.

Methods Related to Both Studies

Procedures

Parents responded to a flyer that was sent home with their children from Head Start or posted at the medical clinic. All families met poverty guidelines based on those reported annually by the U.S. Department of Health and Human Services. Parents received a stipend and the children received a small gift for their participation. All procedures were approved by the Institutional Review Board at each institution and completed only after obtaining written parental consent.

Upon completion of the informed consent process, the parents completed a Parent Information Form and one of two versions of the CBQ (Rothbart, 1996). Children and their parents were recruited as part of larger studies examining attention regulation within the context of poverty. Both the parent and the child completed other measures relevant to the goals of the larger studies that will not be reported here (see Chang & Burns, 2005; Harris et al., 2007).

Data Analysis

To evaluate the validity of using the CBQ to assess temperament in children from low-income families, it is necessary to determine if the 15 dimensions of temperament described by Rothbart, using a sample of children from the general population, cluster into similar factors in children from low-income-families. A principal component analysis of the item scores on the CBQ was used with the extracted factors being obliquely rotated using the Oblimin algorithm (Rothbart, Ahadi et al., 2001).

Study 1
Method

Participants

Participants were 100 children 4-5 years of age ($M = 4.6$ years; $SD = .45$; range 4.03 - 5.6 years). The sample consisted of 49.0% females and 51.0% males with a racial composition as follows: 10% Caucasian and 90% African American. Twenty-three percent of the mothers had less than a high school education, 36% graduated from high school or completed requirements for General Education Degree (GED), and the remaining 41% had some education beyond high school.

Measures

Child temperament. Child temperament was measured using Rothbart's parent-report instrument entitled the Children's Behavior Questionnaire (CBQ; Rothbart,

1996). The CBQ was developed to measure temperament characteristics and is based on the theoretical view that the temperamental processes of arousal, emotion, and self-regulation are key components of human individuality (Derryberry & Rothbart, 1988). Because of the emergent nature of the CBQ, several versions have been reported. In Study 1, we used the 195-item version (Rothbart, Ahadi et al., 2001). The 195 Likert-type items represent the following 15 dimensions of temperament: Activity Level, Anger/Frustration, Approach, Attentional Focusing, Discomfort, Falling Reactivity/Soothability, Fear, High Intensity Pleasure, Impulsivity, Inhibitory Control, Low Intensity Pleasure, Perceptual Sensitivity, Sadness, Shyness, and Smiling and Laughter. Each item is rated by the parent on a scale of 1 (extremely untrue of your child) to 7 (extremely true of your child) or "not applicable (NA)." After re-coding the reverse items, a dimension score was computed by summing all numerical responses and dividing by the number of items in that scale. If an item is omitted or scored as "NA," the sum is divided by the number of completed items.

As previously stated, Rothbart and colleagues (2001) have extracted Effortful Control, Extraversion, and Negative Affect factors from the 15 dimensions. Effortful Control is made up of the dimensions of Attentional Focusing, Inhibitory Control, Low Intensity Pleasure, and Perceptual Sensitivity (Rothbart, Ellis, Rueda, & Posner, 2003). The second factor, Extraversion, is computed from the dimensions of Activity Level, Approach/Anticipation, High Intensity Pleasure, Impulsivity, Shyness (reverse coded), and Smiling and Laughter (Rothbart et al., 2003). Negative Affect, the third factor, is characterized by the dimensions of Anger/Frustration, Discomfort, Falling Reactivity and Soothability (reverse coded), Fear, and Sadness (Rothbart Ahadi et al., 2001).

Rothbart and others have demonstrated agreement between CBQ parent reports and laboratory observational measures of child behavior in typically developing children (Kochanska, Murray, Jacques, Koenig, & Vandergeest, 1996; Rothbart, Ahadi et al., 2001; Rothbart, Derryberry, Reed, & Hershey, 2000). Others have reported similar agreement using other parent-report temperament measures (Matheny, Wilson, & Thoben, 1987).

Demographic data. A researcher-developed parent information questionnaire was used to obtain parent demographic information.

Results

Factor Structure of the 195-item CBQ

The following analyses describe the factor structure in a sample of children from low-income families in the U.S. consistent with Rothbart's findings (Rothbart, Ahadi et al., 2001), three factors were extracted (Table 1). The three factors explained 57.6% of the variance on the 15 temperament dimensions. The dimensions loaded onto the factors in a pattern similar to that in Rothbart's sample, with a few exceptions. Conceptually, Rothbart and colleagues include the dimension of

Smiling and Laughter in the Extraversion factor even though the subscale loaded similarly on both the Extraversion factor (.74) and the Effortful Control factor (.76) in their sample of 4- and 5-year-olds (Rothbart, Ahadi et al., 2001). In the current sample of children, the primary loading for Smiling and Laughter was on Extraversion (.75) with a much smaller coefficient for Effortful Control (.27). In our sample, although different from the sample originally reported by Rothbart, Smiling and Laughter loaded in the manner proposed (Extraversion) in theory by Rothbart and colleagues (Rothbart, Ahadi et al., 2001). The other dimension that varied from Rothbart's sample was Activity Level, which loaded in the following manner: Extraversion (.53) and Effortful Control (.61). In Rothbart's samples (Rothbart, Ahadi et al., 2001), Activity Level clearly loaded on Extraversion.

Table 1

CBQ (195-items) Factor Loadings for Children from Low-Income Families: U.S. Sample of 4- through 5-year-old Children

	Factor		
Scale	1	2	3
	Effortful Control	Negative Affect	Extraversion
Activity level	**-.59**		.53
Anger/frustration		**.73**	
Approach		.29	**.60**
Attention focusing	**.60**		
Discomfort		**.84**	
Falling reactivity/ soothability	.42	**-.61**	
Fear		**.69**	
High intensity pleasure			.75
Impulsivity	-.31		.78
Inhibitory control	**.65**	-.29	
Low Intensity pleasure	**.75**		
Perceptual sensitiv-ity	**.54**		.27
Sadness		**.76**	
Shyness		.42	**-.62**
Smiling/laughter	.26		**.76**

Note. Loadings $\geq$ .25; n = 100

Study 2
Method
Participants

Participants were 215 children 3-7 years of age. The mean age of the children at testing was 5.1 years (*SD* = .98; range 3.2 – 7.6 years). The sample consisted of 53.5% females and 46.5% males with a racial composition as follows: 8.8% Caucasian, 88.4% African American, and 2.8% Other. Twenty-one percent of the mothers had less than a high school education, 30.5% graduated from high school or completed requirements for a GED, and the remaining 48.3% had some education beyond high school.

Measures

Child temperament. Child temperament was measured using Rothbart's 98-item CBQ-short version. The 98 items represent the same 15 dimensions and are rated on the same Likert-type scale as previously described (see Study 1). After the data used for the current study were collected, Rothbart and colleagues revised the CBQ (short version) to its present form of 94 items.
Demographic data. A researcher-developed parent information questionnaire was used to obtain parent demographic information.

Results

Factor Structure of the 98-item CBQ

The following analyses describe the structure in the current sample of children from low-income-families. In Rothbart's normalization study, she had a larger sample and completed factor analyses separately on 3-year-old, 4- to 5-year-old, and 6- to 7-year-old children. The factor structure was similar across the three groups (Rothbart, Ahadi et al., 2001). In the current study, we included data from all children 3 to 7 years of age due to the smaller sample size.

Consistent with Rothbart's findings, three factors were extracted (Table 2). The three factors explained 55.7% of the variance on the 15 temperament dimensions. The dimensions loaded onto the factors in a pattern similar to that in Rothbart, Ahadi et al.'s (2001) sample, with a few exceptions. Conceptually, Rothbart, Ahadi et al. included the dimension of Smiling and Laughter in the Extraversion factor even though the subscale loaded similarly on both the Extraversion (.74) and the Effortful Control (.76) factors in their sample of 4- and 5-year-olds. In the current sample of children, again, the primary loading for Smiling and Laughter was on Effortful Control (.69), but with a much smaller coefficient for Extraversion (.28). The dimension that varied the most from that of the normalization sample was the dimension of Inhibitory Control, which loaded in the following manner: Extraversion (-.56), Effortful Control (.48), and Negative Affect (-.44). In Rothbart's samples, Inhibitory Control also loads on all three factors, but the highest loading is on Effortful Control rather than Extraversion (See Rothbart, Ahadi et al.).

Table 2

CBQ (98-items) Factor Loadings for Children from Low-Income Families: U.S. Sample of 3- through 7-year-old Children

Scale	Factor		
	1	2	3
	Effortful Control	Negative Affect	Extraversion
Activity level			**.80**
Anger/frustration		**.74**	.37
Approach		.39	**.59**
Attention focusing	**.70**		-.36
Discomfort		**.69**	
Falling reactivity/ soothability	-.41	**.63**	
Fear		**.57**	-.36
High intensity pleasure			**.67**
Impulsivity			**.79**
Inhibitory control	.48	-.44	**-.56**
Low Intensity pleasure	**.69**		
Perceptual sensitiv- ity	**.73**		
Sadness		**.76**	
Shyness		-.29	**.43**
Smiling/laughter	**.69**		.28

Note. Loadings $\geq$ .25; $n = 215$

Discussion

Children from low-income families are at higher risk for a variety of behavioral and academic problems; however, there exists meaningful individual differences within the population (Brooks-Gunn et al., 2005; Brooks-Gunn et al., 2007). These demonstrated differences, in the face of very similar risk factors, have spurred researchers to examine child factors that may relate to later developmental outcomes. Temperament is one such child factor that also shows considerable individual differences and has been associated with academic and behavioral functioning in children (Bates et al., 1998; Lengua, 2002). The current study examines temperament in the context of poverty by comparing the factor structure of the CBQ in a sample of children from low-income households with Rothbart's original samples.

Rothbart's model of temperament includes 15 dimensions that are grouped into three factors, Effortful Control, Extraversion, and Negative Affect. This factor structure has been generally confirmed in samples of Chinese (Ahadi et al., 1993; Bates et al., 1998; Lengua, 2002) and Japanese children (Kusangi, 1993 as cited in Rothbart et al., 2001) as well as children born prematurely (Davis et al., 2006). The current findings further extend the previously observed factor structure to two samples of low-income children, with a few exceptions. The most striking deviation occurred in the dimension of inhibitory control. In the current sample, inhibitory control loaded on all three factors, with the highest loading on Extraversion. In contrast, although items in Rothbart's normalization samples also loaded on all three factors, the highest loading occurred on Effortful Control. These samples were mostly comprised of middle- to upper-class, white participants. However, when testing the reliability and validity of a short and very short version of the CBQ, Putnam and Rothbart (2006) included data sets of African American and low-income participants. When looking at only those groups, it was found that internal consistency of scales substantially decreased.

One possible explanation given by Putnam and Rothbart (2006) for these findings involved sensitivity to different subcultural dialects. That is, it could be possible that individuals with different dialects within low-income or African American subcultures interpret questionnaire items differently than individuals who are white or who are more affluent (Gopaul-McNicol, Reid, & Wisdom, 1998; Putnam & Rothbart, 2006). In developing items on the CBQ, Rothbart and colleagues used statements from the latter populations. If there are, in fact, sub-cultural, dialectical differences within low-income populations, this could account for deviations in the way they are answering questions.

In contrast to Putnam and Rothbart's (2006) findings with children from low-income households, however, Blair and Razza (2007) found acceptable levels of internal consistency in a sample of 141 children from Head Start. In addition, they did not find the inhibitory control difference that was demonstrated in the factor-loading pattern of the current study. It is notable that their sample was predominantly Caucasian, with only 2% of the sample comprising African Americans compared to almost 90% in our sample. Thus, it could be that our findings were specific to African Americans or African Americans living in poverty.

Alternatively, there could be qualitative differences in the inhibitory control of children from low-income families relative to their higher-income peers. Inhibitory control, in particular, has recently been associated with several measures of academic performance, including math and reading ability (Blair & Razza, 2007). Inhibitory control has been viewed as the core of children's developing executive function (Diamond, Kirkham, & Amso, 2002). Perhaps the varying academic performance within children of poverty is related to individual differences in executive function and, specifically, inhibitory control. Moreover, in fact, self-regulatory skills, including executive function, have been linked to differing outcomes for children of poverty (Buckner, Mezzacappa, & Beardslee, 2003).

Overall, our results suggest that the CBQ is an appropriate instrument for measuring temperament in children from low-income families. However, further investigation is warranted. As described above, a previous study reported decreased internal consistency in the short and very short forms in this population (Putnam & Rothbart, 2006). Additionally, the current findings indicate deviations from the standard factor-loading pattern in the dimension of inhibitory control. Lastly, future samples should further examine whether observed differences can be better attributed to race or income level.

References

Ackerman, B. P., Brown, E. D., & Izard, C. E. (2004). The relation between contextual risk, earned income, and the school adjustment of children from economically disadvantaged families. *Developmental Psychology, 40*, 204-216.

Ahadi, S. A., Rothbart, M. K., & Ye, R. M. (1993). Children's temperament in the U.S. and China: Similarities and differences. *European Journal of Personality, 7*, 359-377.

Bates, J. E., Dodge, K. A., Pettit, G. S., & Ridge, B. (1998). Interaction of temperamental resistance to control and restrictive parenting in the development of existing behavior. *Developmental Psychology, 34*, 982-995.

Blair, C., & Razza, R. P. (2007). Relating effortful control, executive function, and false belief understanding to emerging math and literacy ability in kindergarten. *Child Development, 78*, 647-663.

Brooks-Gunn, J., Klebanov, P. K., & Duncan, G. (1996). Ethnic differences in children's intelligence test scores: Role of economic deprivation, home environment, and maternal characteristics. *Child Development, 64*, 736-753.

Brooks-Gunn, J., Linver, M. R., & Fauth, R. C. (2005). Children's competence and socioeconomic status in the family and neighborhood. In A. J. Elliot & C. S. Dweck (Eds.), *Handbook of competence and motivation* (pp. 414-435). New York: Guilford Press.

Brooks-Gunn, J., Rouse, C. E., & McLanahan, S. (2007). Racial and ethnic gaps in school readiness. In R. C. Pianta, M. J. Cox, & K. L. Snow (Eds.), *School readiness & the transition to kindergarten in the era of accountability* (pp. 283-306). Baltimore, MD: Brookes.

Buckner, J. C., Mezzacappa, E., & Beardslee, W. R. (2003). Characteristics of resilient youths living in poverty: The role of self-regulatory processes. *Development and Psychopathology, 15*, 139-162.

Cairns, R. B., Cairns, B. D., & Neckerman, H. J. (1989). Early school dropout: Configurations and determinants. *Child Development, 60*, 1437-1452.

Campbell, F. A., & Ramey, C. T. (1994). Effects of early intervention on intellectual and academic achievement: A follow-up study of children from low-income families. *Child Development, 65*, 684-698.

Chang, F., & Burns, B. M. (2005). Attention in preschoolers: Associations with effortful control and motivation. *Child Development, 76*, 247-263.

Davis, D. W., Chang, F., & Burns, B. M. (2006). An evaluation of the Children's Behavior Questionnaire for use with very low birth weight preschoolers. *Journal of Early Childhood and Infant Psychology, 2*, 181-200.

Derryberry, D., & Rothbart, M. K. (1988). Arousal, affect, and attention as components of temperament. *Journal of Personality and Social Psychology, 55*, 958-966.

Diamond, A., Kirkham, N., & Amso, D. (2002). Conditions under which young children can hold two rules in mind and inhibit a prepotent response. *Developmental Psychology, 38*, 352-362.

Gopaul-McNicol, S., Reid, G., & Wisdom, C. (1998). The psychoeducational assessment of ebonics speakers: Issues and challenges. *Journal of Negro Education, 67*, 16–24.

Harris, R. C., Robinson, J. B., Chang, F., & Burns, B. M. (2007). Characterizing preschool children's attention regulation in parent-child interactions: The roles of effortful control and motivation. *Journal of Applied Developmental Psychology, 28*, 25-39.

Janosz, M., Le Blanc, M., Boulerice, B., & Tremblay, R. E. (2000). Predicting different types of school dropouts: A typological approach with two longitudinal samples. *Journal of Educational Psychology, 92*, 171-190.

Kane, T. J. (1998). Racial and ethnic preferences in college admissions. In C. Jencks & M. Phillips (Eds.), *The black-white test score gap* (pp. 431-456). Washington, DC: Brookings Institute Press.

Kochanska, G., Murray, K., Jacques, T. Y., Koenig, A. L., & Vandergeest, K. A. (1996). Inhibitory control in young children and its role in emerging internalization. *Child Development, 67*, 490-507.

Kusanagi, E. (1993). A psychometric examination of the Child Behavior Questionnaire. In *Annual Report 1991-1992, No. 15*. Sapporo, Japan: Hokkaido University.

Lengua, L. (2002). The contribution of emotionality and self-regulation to the understanding of children's response to multiple risk. *Child Development, 73*(1), 144-161.

Li-Grining, C. P. (2007). Effortful control among low-income preschoolers in three cities: Stability, change, and individual differences. *Developmental*

Psychology, 43, 208-221.

Martini, T. S., Root, C. A., & Jenkins, J. M. (2004). Low and middle income mothers' regulation of negative emotion: Effects of children's temperament and situational emotional responses. *Social Development, 13*, 515-530.

Matheny, A. P., Wilson, R. S., & Thoben, A. S. (1987). Home and mother: Relations with infant temperament. *Developmental Pyschology, 23*(3), 323-331.

Nygaard, E., Smith, L., & Torgersen, A. M. (2002). Temperament in children with Down syndrome and in prematurely born children. *Scandinavian Journal of Psychology, 43*, 61-71.

Orr, A. J. (2003). Black-white differences in achievement: The importance of wealth. *Sociology of Education, 76*, 281-304.

Putnam, S. P., & Rothbart, M. K. (2006). Development of short and very short forms of the Children's Behavior Questionnaire. *Child Development, 87*, 103-113.

Ramey, C. T., & Campbell, F. A. (1991). Poverty, early childhood education, and academic competence: The Abecedarian experiment. In A. Huston (Ed.), *Children reared in poverty* (pp. 190-221). New York: Cambridge University Press.

Rothbart, M. K. (1996). *Children's Behavior Questionnaire*. Oregon: University of Oregon.

Rothbart, M. K., Ahadi, S. A., & Evans, D. E. (2000). Temperament and personality: Origins and outcomes. *Journal of Personality and Social Psychology, 78*, 122-135.

Rothbart, M. K., Ahadi, S. A., Hershey, K. L., & Fisher, P. (2001). Investigations of temperament at three to seven years: The Children's Behavior Questionnaire. *Child Development, 72*, 1394-1408.

Rothbart, M.K., & Bates, J.E. (1998). Temperament. In W. Damon (Ed.), *Handbook of child psychology* (5th ed., Vol. 3, pp. 105-176). New York: Wiley.

Rothbart, M. K., Chew, K. H., & Gartstein, M. A. (2001). Assessment of temperament in early development. In L. T. Singer & P. S. Zeskind (Eds.), *Biobehavioral assessment of the infant* (pp. 190-208). New York: Guilford Press.

Rothbart, M. K., & Derryberry, D. (1981). Development of individual differences in temperament. In M. E. Lamb & A. L. Brown (Eds.), *Advances in developmental psychology* (Vol. 1, pp. 37-86). Hillsdale, NJ: Erlbaum.

Rothbart, M. K., Derryberry, D., Reed, M. A., & Hershey, K. (2000). Stability of temperament in childhood: Laboratory infant assessment to parent report at seven years. In D. L. Molfese & V. J. Molfese (Eds.), *Temperament and personality development across the life span* (pp. 85-119). Hillsdale: NJ: Erlbaum.

Rothbart, M. K., Ellis, L. K., Rueda, M. R., & Posner, M. I. (2003). Developing mechanisms of temperamental effortful control. *Journal of Personality, 71*, 1113-1143.

Thomas, A., Chess, S., Birch, H. G., Hertzig, M. E., & Korn, S. (1963). *Behavioral individuality in early childhood.* New York: New York University Press.

Erratum

Authorship for "Infant and Child Attachment as it Relates to School-Based Outcomes" (*JECIP*, Volume 3, pp. 47-60) originally listed as Kehle, T. J., Bray, M. A., & Grigerick should be Kehle, T. J., Bray, M. A., Grigerick, S., Nicholson, H., & Foote, C.